ONLY YOUR LOVE
and
YOUR GRACE

ONLY YOUR LOVE
and
YOUR GRACE

On Directing the Spiritual Exercises
of St. Ignatius of Loyola

Robert Fabing, SJ

Paulist Press

New York / Mahwah, NJ

All quotations from the text of the Spiritual Exercises are from *The Spiritual Exercises of St. Ignatius, A New Translation Based on Studies in the Language of the Autograph*, translated by Louis J. Puhl, SJ (Westminster, MD: Newman Press, 1951).

Cover image by lunamarina / Shutterstock.com
Cover design by Joe Gallagher
Book design by Lynn Else

Library of Congress Cataloging-in-Publication Data
Names: Fabing, Robert, 1942– author.
Title: Only your love and your grace : on directing the spiritual exercises of St. Ignatius of Loyola / Robert Fabing.
Description: New York : Paulist Press, [2021] | Includes bibliographical references. | Summary: "Only Your Love and Your Grace is a guidebook for directors with experience giving the Spiritual Exercises, but who will benefit from the author's deep experience of walking with retreatants through the full thirty-day retreat. Directors can gain from this an appreciation for the art and grace of the Spiritual Exercises in a new way, and retreatants, too, will see their experience in a new light"—Provided by publisher.
Identifiers: LCCN 2020037165 (print) | LCCN 2020037166 (ebook) | ISBN 9780809154913 (paperback) | ISBN 9781587688874 (ebook)
Subjects: LCSH: Ignatius, of Loyola, Saint, 1491–1556. Exercitia spiritualia. | Spiritual exercises. | Spiritual retreats—Catholic Church. | Spiritual life—Catholic Church.
Classification: LCC BX2179.L8 F325 2021 (print) | LCC BX2179.L8 (ebook) | DDC 248.3—dc23
LC record available at https://lccn.loc.gov/2020037165
LC ebook record available at https://lccn.loc.gov/2020037166

ISBN 978-0-8091-5491-3 (paperback)
ISBN 987-1-58768-887-4 (e-book)

Published by Paulist Press
997 Macarthur Boulevard
Mahwah, New Jersey 07430
www.paulistpress.com

Printed and bound in the
United States of America

Dedicated in Memoriam
to
Father Lawrence E. Boadt, CSP
(1942–2010)
my publisher
and to
Father Howard J. Gray, SJ
(1930–2018)
my spiritual director for many years

CONTENTS

CONTENTS

PREFACE

ST. IGNATIUS LOYOLA died in 1556. In the years since, countless books have been written about his Spiritual Exercises. I present the following reflections from having given the full thirty-day Spiritual Exercises of St. Ignatius of Loyola every year for forty-four years.

This book has come from those years of experience. My desire is that after the thirty days, a retreatants cannot remember their director's name, as they know that Christ was their Director. I hope this work will engender volumes in the ensuing years.

Robert Fabing, SJ
Jesuit Retreat Center
Los Altos, California

ACKNOWLEDGMENTS

I WOULD LIKE to thank and remember all my fellow directors over the years and all the directors here at the Jesuit Retreat Center in Los Altos, California. Also, I would like to thank Mrs. Cris Goodman for her typing skills in preparing this work.

INTRODUCTION
The Act of the Presence of God

As we begin, I would like to call attention to the foundations of the Spiritual Exercises of St. Ignatius Loyola. All prayer, for Ignatius, begins with the "Act of the Presence of God." Unfortunately, the Act of the Presence of God is the most misunderstood prayer exercise in ascetical and prayer history.

The Act is not standing or kneeling before you pray and experiencing God's Presence. The Act has nothing to do with the retreatant's "feeling" God's Presence (one could be there for ten hours and not feel God's Presence). The Act of the Presence is about *God feeling you.* God is looking at you, the retreatant, as you begin to pray. *You* are in God's Presence, simply resting in the fact that God is beholding you, not that you are beholding God. So simply rest in being beheld. A simple reading of Psalm 139, which speaks of God's intimate knowledge of us, will highlight this exercise:

> O LORD, you have searched me and known me.
> You know when I sit down and when I rise up;
>   you discern my thoughts from far away. (vv. 1–2)

ONLY YOUR LOVE and YOUR GRACE

My aim in this book is to

- Ensure that the experience of the retreatants with their Creator and Lord is primary;
- Establish a clear idea of what St. Ignatius means in the Exercises;
- Establish the signs of when an individual is asking for the grace of the next exercise, and the material;
- Look at methods and ways, including technology, of delivering the Spiritual Exercises of St. Ignatius to a retreatant.

My hope in doing this is to produce in others the art of giving the Spiritual Exercises.

FIRST WEEK

Chapter 1

THE FIRST PRINCIPLE AND FOUNDATION

From the text of the Spiritual Exercises of St. Ignatius of Loyola:

21. SPIRITUAL EXERCISES

Which have as their purpose the conquest of self and the regulation of one's life in such a way that no decision is made under the influence of any inordinate attachment.

PRESUPPOSITION

22. To assure better cooperation between the one who is giving the Exercises and the exercitant, and more beneficial results for both, it is necessary to suppose that every good Christian is more ready to put a good interpretation on another's statement than to condemn it as false. If an orthodox construction cannot be put on a proposition, the one who made it should be asked how he understands it. If he is in error, he should be corrected with all kindness. If this does not suffice, all appropriate means should be used to bring him to a correct interpretation, and so defend the proposition from error.

23. FIRST PRINCIPLE AND FOUNDATION

Man is created to praise, reverence, and serve God our Lord, and by this means to save his soul.

The other things on the face of the earth are created for man to help him in attaining the end for which he is created.

Hence, man is to make use of them in as far as they help him in the attainment of his end, and he must rid himself of them in as far as they prove a hindrance to him.

Therefore, we must make ourselves indifferent to all created things, as far as we are allowed free choice and are not under any prohibition. Consequently, as far as we are concerned, we should not prefer health to sickness, riches to poverty, honor to dishonor, a long life to a short life. The same holds for all other things.

Our one desire and choice should be what is more conducive to the end for which we are created.

43. METHOD OF MAKING THE GENERAL EXAMINATION OF CONSCIENCE

There are five points in this method:

1. The first point is to give thanks to God our Lord for the favors received.
2. The second point is to ask for grace to know my sins and to rid myself of them.
3. The third point is to demand an account of my soul from the time of rising up to the present examination. I should go over one hour after another, one period after another. The thoughts should be examined first, then the words, and finally, the deeds in the same order as was explained under the Particular Examination of Conscience.
4. The fourth point will be to ask pardon of God our Lord for my faults.

5. The fifth point will be to resolve to amend with the grace of God. Close with an *Our Father.*

44. GENERAL CONFESSION AND HOLY COMMUNION

Among many advantages of a general confession which one makes of his own accord during the time of the Spiritual Exercises, there are especially these three:

1. It is true that one who confesses every year has no obligation to make a general confession. But if one is made, there will be much greater merit and profit because of the greater sorrow experienced for all the sins and perversities of his whole life.

2. While one is going through the Spiritual Exercises, a far deeper insight into his sins and their malice is acquired than at a time when he is not so engaged with what concerns his inner life. Since at this time he attains to a deeper knowledge and sorrow for his sins, there will be greater profit and merit than he would otherwise have had.

3. As a consequence of having made a better confession, and of being better disposed, he will find that he is more worthy and better prepared to receive the Most Blessed Sacrament. This reception will strengthen him not only against falling into sin but will also help him to retain the increase of grace which he has gained.

It will be better to make this general confession immediately after the Exercises of the First Week.

THE FIRST PRINCIPLE AND FOUNDATION: FACT AND PRACTICE

God freely created us so that we might know, love, and serve Him in this life and be happy with Him forever. God's purpose in creating us is to draw forth from us a response of love and service here on earth, so that we may attain our goal of everlasting happiness with Him in heaven.

All the things in this world are gifts of God, created for us, to be the means by which we can come to know Him better, love Him more surely, and serve Him more faithfully.

In everyday life, then, we should keep ourselves indifferent or undecided in the face of all created gifts when we have an option and we do not have the clarity of what would be a better choice. We ought not to be led only by our natural likes and dislikes even in matters such as health or sickness, wealth, or poverty, between living in the East or in the West, becoming an accountant or a lawyer.

Rather, our only desire and our one choice should be that option that better leads us to the goal for which God created us.

> **Note:** This consideration is to be read over by the retreatant a
> few times each day during the first few days of the retreat. As
> is evident, these words express the basic Christian catechesis
> in the general terms of salvation. The prayer of the retreatant
> at this time may well be guided by scriptural texts that
> will enlighten and reinforce the notions contained in this
> foundation.

St. Ignatius's First Principle and Foundation is not a meditation, nor is it a contemplation in his Spiritual Exercises. Actually, it is not meant to be an isolated one-hour prayer time. It is a consideration retreatants are meant to have as an ambience to "consider" during the opening day of the full thirty-day Spiritual Exercises. It is meant to be a background as a person begins, to be read over during the opening day as a retreatant enters into the retreat.

What is the grace of the First Principle and Foundation?

What is this? What is it saying? How do you handle it?

- The First Principle and Foundation is a consideration.

- ◆ The "choice" is an act of the will…a decision.
- ◆ To "make ourselves indifferent" is a choice. "Indifference" is a choice…not a feeling…not an affect.
- ◆ "Indifference" is a willingness to be purposeful. Retreatants are to be unbiased as to a "means."

- Our purpose in life is central and all else is only an expression of our purpose.

  - ◆ Our image of God is as Creator…all else is what God has created.
  - ◆ By praising God, we will become what God wants us to become.
  - ◆ God's plan is different for each person.

- What will release the grip of "attachments"? Only love of God—only a deeper affection—can order disordered affections.

  - ◆ The grace is the freedom to choose.
  - ◆ What creates this freedom?
  - ◆ A "means" is only a means. It is not an "end." So a means can influence—but it cannot be decisive. Only God's movement in the First Principle and Foundation is the decisive element of decision-making…so all else is simply all else.
  - ◆ A means is influential but not determinative in a choice.
  - ◆ An idol is a means that is treated as an end. This is the meaning of idolatry.

- Indifference is a necessary grace and disposition for a choice.

  - ◆ Indifference is not a sense of affection—it is a "choosing."
  - ◆ Sickness or health does not stop me from my end, which is praising and serving God. I can do that no matter how rich or poor I am.

- ◆ So, means here are differentiated from my end.

- The First Principle and Foundation is the purpose of my existence…and gives me my RELATIONSHIP to all things.

  - ◆ The First Principle and Foundation sets up a program of action for choosing and doing.
  - ◆ The First Principle and Foundation is a program.
  - ◆ The First Principle and Foundation is countercultural, as culture is a means; the First Principle and Foundation is deeper than culture.
  - ◆ If I don't use things correctly for my end, I don't use creation for the end for which it was created.
  - ◆ The First Principle and Foundation is an ascetical goal—if you attained it, you wouldn't need the Spiritual Exercises.

- Christ is correcting the way I think about myself in the First Principle and Foundation.

  - ◆ **Theologically:** a human person is created by God.
  - ◆ **Cosmologically:** God created every person and the whole world.
  - ◆ **Teleologically:** all reality is going to God.
  - ◆ **Ethically:** This is a method: of choosing.
  - ◆ **Psychologically:** Paragraph 4 of the First Principle and Foundation says, "We must make ourselves indifferent to all created things." This is a signpost. If the retreatants can relate to this, then send them on to the rest of the retreat.

- Like Beethoven's Ninth Symphony, the theme gets deeper in the kingdom, then the "Two Standards," then the "Three Degrees of Humility."
- This is a holistic view. Indifference is to stay in the present moment because I think that if I go in one direction "this or that will happen," and none of that may be true.

The First Principle and Foundation should lead to an openness to deepen itself in a person and a desire to proceed to get it.

- The First Principle and Foundation is a compass—a direction toward true north—giving the gauge of a person, an image of God or of oneself.
- *What* really matters to a person?
- *Who* really matters to a person?
- St. Ignatius wrote the First Principle and Foundation ten years after Manresa because he needed a screening process to save him time finding out whether a person was capable of doing the Spiritual Exercises.
- What is your horizon of being? God? Or "an experience" or "a thing" or "a creature"?
- You have here a method criticizing the "means" at hand… the First Principle and Foundation is a method of criticism.
- Does your experience sit on the "horizon of God"? In the present moment?
- Do you have a method of criticizing the means at hand? From another viewpoint?

The First Principle and Foundation grace is…

…an acknowledgment that this is the direction the retreatant should and wants to be going in, not an attainment of it.

- The desire for chocolate will never go away until two minutes after a person who likes chocolate is dead. So the First Principle and Foundation is not going to change that. It is meant to move in the direction of freedom and separation from that desire, not to eradicate the desire, which will never happen.
- "Man is created to praise, reverence, and serve God our Lord, and by this means to save his soul" (Exercises 23).

- "Man" here is everyone, both men and women.
- This praise comes from an appreciation of who God is and God's gifts in creation.
- This sense comes from a sense of thanksgiving.

What are the signs a person is asking for the first principle and foundation?

When a retreatant says something like the following:

- I'm experiencing a deep desire for God, the love of God, that relegates all else to be "all else." All else is secondary.
- I want to want this.
- I'm experiencing a general sense that I have lost my priorities.
- I need to center.
- My relations are askew.
- I have to find a vision again.
- I want a sense of inner freedom again.
- I want a sense of thanksgiving again.
- I want to give all to God.
- I need a balance in my life.
- I need a perspective that I don't have.
- There is a void in my life, and I need to fill it.
- I want the joy of giving all to God again.
- I want the innocence of giving all to God again.
- I want my innocence back.
- I'm apprehensive but I want to enter in.
- I'm scattered—I want to be focused.
- I'm not sure where my life is going.
- Things are going okay, but something is missing. I want more.
- I want the sense of God I had and lost.
- I have been crying over the wasted years of my life.

- I'm seeing and experiencing a sense that my life has been wasted on "this or that"—everything in my life has been Godless.
- I have a deep yearning to have God be primary.
- I need perspective in my life.
- I've been wondering where I'm going.
- I want God to be a greater part of my life.
- I want my purity back.
- I'm very peaceful, and I'm experiencing in my prayer an ability to reflect, which is unique for me.
- There is in me a deep dissatisfaction I have not explored—a vague tension to ask a question.
- You know, I'm experiencing myself as free enough to look at and, maybe, overcome my fear.
- You know, I've lost my freedom.

HOW DO YOU GIVE THE FIRST PRINCIPLE AND FOUNDATION?

1. Read it aloud. Put it on your dresser…reading it and considering it.
2. Scriptures from among these will apply:
   - Genesis 1:26–31, *the creation*
   - Colossians 1:15–20, *Christ, the Head of creation*
   - Wisdom 9:1–18, *Solomon's choice of wisdom first*
   - Jeremiah 18, *the potter and the clay*
   - Deuteronomy 30:1–15, *God's faithfulness assured*
   - Psalm 104, *God, Creator of all*
   - Deuteronomy 7:1–11, *a sinful yet chosen people*
   - Psalm 8, *divine majesty and human dignity*
   - Ephesians 1, *spiritual blessings in Christ*
   - Matthew 22:37; Luke 10:27; see also Deuteronomy 6:5, *Jesus's Great Commandment*: You must love the Lord

your God with all your heart, with all your soul, and with all your strength.

3. Ask yourself two questions about giving the First Principle and Foundation:

- What is my purpose?
- What am I about?

Direction in and within the Spiritual Exercises...

IS **NOT**

- The gift of teaching; it is not a lecture, not preaching or exhortation, and not prophecy.
- The gift of counseling:
  - ◆ You may be able to see something in a person, but God may not want the retreatant to go there.
  - ◆ It is not psychological counseling.
- Spiritual direction such as outside the Spiritual Exercises, where that would be worthy and advisable.

As a director, simply ask, What did God say to you? and, How did it make you feel?

The 15th Annotation applies here:

He who is giving the Exercises ought not to influence him who is receiving them more to poverty or to a promise, than to their opposites, nor more to one state or way of life than to another. For though, outside the Exercises, we can lawfully and with merit influence everyone who is probably fit to choose continence, virginity, the religious life and all manner of evangelical perfection, still in the Spiritual Exercises, when seeking the Divine Will, it is more fitting and much better, that the Creator and Lord Himself should communicate Himself to His devout soul, inflaming it with His love and praise, and disposing it for the way in which it will be better able to serve Him in future. So, he who is giving the Exercises should not turn or incline to one side or the other, but standing in the center like a balance, leave the Creator to act immediately with the creature, and the creature with its Creator and Lord.

Chapter 2

THE FIRST WEEK OF THE SPIRITUAL EXERCISES

From the text of the Spiritual Exercises of St. Ignatius of Loyola:

45. FIRST EXERCISE

> *This is a meditation on the first, second and third sin employing the three powers of the soul. After the preparatory prayer and two preludes, it contains three principal points and a colloquy.*

46. PRAYER. In the preparatory prayer I will beg God our Lord for grace that all my intentions, actions, and operations may be directed purely to the praise and service of His Divine Majesty.

47. FIRST PRELUDE. This is a mental representation of the place.

Attention must be called to the following point. When the contemplation or meditation is on something visible, for example, when we contemplate Christ our Lord, the representation will consist in seeing in imagination the material place where the object is that we wish to contemplate. I said the material place, for example, the temple, or the mountain where Jesus or His Mother is, according to the subject matter of the contemplation.

In a case where the subject matter is not visible, as here in a meditation on sin, the representation will be to see in imagination my soul as a prisoner in this corruptible body, and to consider my whole composite being as an exile here on earth, cast out to live among brute beasts. I said my whole composite being, body and soul.

48. THE SECOND PRELUDE. I will ask God our Lord for what I want and desire.

The petition made in this prelude must be according to the subject matter. Thus in a contemplation on the Resurrection I will ask for joy with Christ in joy. In one on the passion, I will ask for sorrow, tears, and anguish with Christ in anguish.

Here it will be to ask for shame and confusion, because I see how many have been lost on account of a single mortal sin, and how many times I have deserved eternal damnation because of the many grievous sins that I have committed.

49. *Note*

The Preparatory Prayer, which is never changed, and the two Preludes mentioned above, which are changed at times according to the subject matter, must always be made before all the contemplations and meditations.

50. THE FIRST POINT. This will consist in using the memory to recall the first sin, which was that of the angels, and then in applying the understanding by reasoning upon this sin, then the will by seeking to remember and understand all to be the more filled with shame and confusion when I compare the one

sin of the angels with the many sins I have committed. I will consider that they went to hell for one sin, and the number of times I have deserved to be condemned forever because of my numerous sins.

I said we should apply the memory to the sin of the angels, that is, recalling that they were created in the state of grace, that they did not want to make use of the freedom God gave them to reverence and obey their Creator and Lord, and so falling into pride, were changed from grace to hatred of God, and cast out of heaven into hell.

So, too, the understanding is to be used to think over the matter more in detail, and then the will to rouse more deeply the emotions.

51. SECOND POINT. In the same way the three powers of the soul are to be applied to the sin of Adam and Eve. Recall to memory how on account of this sin they did penance for so long a time, and the great corruption which came upon the human race that caused so many to be lost in hell.

I said recall to mind the second sin, that of our First Parents. After Adam had been created on the Plain of Damascus and placed in the Garden of Paradise, and Eve had been formed from his side, they sinned by violating the command not to eat of the tree of knowledge. Thereafter, they were clothed in garments of skin and cast out of Paradise. By their sin they lost original justice, and for the rest of their lives, lived without it in many labors and great penance.

So, too, the understanding is to be used to think over the matter in greater detail, and the will is to be used as explained above.

52. THIRD POINT. In like manner, we are to do the same with regard to the third sin, namely, that of one who went to hell

because of one mortal sin. Consider also countless others who have been lost for fewer sins than I have committed.

I said to do the same for the third particular sin. Recall to memory the gravity and malice of sin against our Creator and Lord. Use the understanding to consider that because of sin, and of acting against the Infinite Goodness, one is justly condemned forever. Close with the acts of the will as we have said above.

53. COLLOQUY. Imagine Christ our Lord present before you upon the cross, and begin to speak with him, asking how it is that though He is the Creator, He has stooped to become man, and to pass from eternal life to death here in time, that thus He might die for our sins.

I shall also reflect upon myself and ask:

"What have I done for Christ?" "What am I doing for Christ?" "What ought I to do for Christ?"

As I behold Christ in this plight, nailed to the cross, I shall ponder upon what presents itself to my mind.

54. *Note on Colloquies*

The colloquy is made by speaking exactly as one friend speaks to another, or as a servant speaks to a master, now asking him for a favor, now blaming himself for some misdeed, now making known his affairs to him, and seeking advice in them. Close with an *Our Father*.

55. SECOND EXERCISE

This is a meditation on our sins. After the preparatory prayer and two preludes there are five points and a colloquy

PRAYER. The preparatory prayer will be the same.

FIRST WEEK

First Prelude. This will be the same as in the First Exercise.

Second Prelude. This is to ask for what I desire. Here it will be to ask for a growing and intense sorrow and tears for my sins.

56. First Point. This is the record of my sins. I will call to mind all the sins of my life, reviewing year by year, and period by period. Three things will help me in this: First, to consider the place where I lived; secondly, my dealings with others; thirdly, the office I have held.

57. Second Point. I will weigh the gravity of my sins and see the loathsomeness and malice which every mortal sin I have committed has in itself, even though it were not forbidden.

58. Third Point. I will consider who I am, and by means of examples humble myself:

1. What am I compared with all men?
2. What are all men compared with the angels and saints of paradise?
3. Consider what all creation is in comparison with God. Then I alone, what can I be?
4. I will consider all the corruption and loathsomeness of my body.
5. I will consider myself as a source of corruption and contagion from which has issued countless sins and evils and the most offensive poison.

59. Fourth Point. I will consider who God is against whom I have sinned, going through His attributes and comparing them with their contraries in me: His wisdom with my ignorance, His power with my weakness, His justice with my iniquity, His goodness with my wickedness.

60. FIFTH POINT. This is a cry of wonder accompanied by surging emotion as I pass in review all creatures. How is it that they have permitted me to live and have sustained me in life! Why have the angels, though they are the sword of God's justice, tolerated me, guarded me, and prayed for me! Why have the saints interceded for me and asked favors for me! And the heavens, sun, moon, stars, and the elements; the fruits, birds, fishes, and other animals—why have they all been at my service! How is it that the earth did not open to swallow me up and create new hells in which I should be tormented forever!

61. COLLOQUY. I will conclude with a colloquy, extolling the mercy of God our Lord, pouring out my thoughts to Him, and giving thanks to Him that up to this very moment He has granted me life. I will resolve with His grace to amend for the future. Close with an *Our Father*.

62. THIRD EXERCISE

This is a repetition of the first and second exercises with three colloquies

After the preparatory prayer and the two preludes, this exercise will consist in repeating the First and Second Exercises. In doing this, we should pay attention to and dwell upon those points in which we have experienced greater consolation or desolation or greater spiritual appreciation. After the repetition, three colloquies are to be used in the following manner:

63. FIRST COLLOQUY. The first colloquy will be with our Blessed Lady, that she may obtain grace for me from her Son and Lord for three favors:

1. A deep knowledge of my sins and a feeling of abhorrence for them;
2. An understanding of the disorder of my actions, that filled with horror of them, I may amend my life and put it in order;
3. A knowledge of the world, that filled with horror, I may put away from me all that is worldly and vain.

Then I will say a *Hail Mary.*

SECOND COLLOQUY. I will make the same petitions to her Son that He may obtain these graces from the Father for me.

After that I will say *Soul of Christ.*

THIRD COLLOQUY. I will make the same requests of the Father that He Himself, the eternal Lord, may grant them to me.

Then I will close with the *Our Father.*

64. FOURTH EXERCISE

This exercise consists of a summary of the third exercise given above

I have called it a summary because the intellect, without any digression, diligently thinks over and recalls the matter contemplated in the previous exercises. The same three colloquies should be used at the close.

65. FIFTH EXERCISE

This is a meditation on hell. Besides the preparatory prayer and two preludes it contains five points and a colloquy

PRAYER. The preparatory prayer will be as usual.

FIRST PRELUDE. This is a representation of the place. Here it will be to see in imagination the length, breadth, and depth of hell.

SECOND PRELUDE. I should ask for what I desire. Here it will be to beg for a deep sense of the pain which the lost suffer, that if because of my faults I forget the love of the eternal Lord, at least the fear of these punishments will keep me from falling into sin.

66. FIRST POINT. This will be to see in imagination the vast fires, and the souls enclosed, as it were, in bodies of fire.

67. SECOND POINT. To hear the wailing, the howling, cries, and blasphemies against Christ our Lord and against His saints.

68. THIRD POINT. With the sense of smell to perceive the smoke, the sulfur, the filth, and corruption.

69. FOURTH POINT. To taste the bitterness of tears, sadness, and remorse of conscience.

70. FIFTH POINT. With the sense of touch to feel the flames which envelop and burn the souls.

71. COLLOQUY. Enter into conversation with Christ our Lord. Recall to memory that of those who are in hell, some came there because they did not believe in the coming of Christ; others, though they believed, because they did not keep the Commandments. Divide them all into three classes:

1. Those who were lost before the coming of Christ;
2. Those who were lost during His lifetime;
3. Those who were lost after His life here on earth.

Thereupon, I will give thanks to God our Lord that He has not put an end to my life and permitted me to fall into any of these three classes.

I shall also thank Him for this, that up to this very moment He has shown Himself so loving and merciful to me.

Close with an *Our Father.*

(OTHER EXERCISES)

(If the one giving the Exercises judges that it would be profitable for the exercitant, other exercises may be added here, for example, on death and other punishments of sin, on judgment, etc. Let him not think this is forbidden, though they are not given here.)

72. *Note*

The First Exercise will be made at midnight; the Second, immediately on rising in the morning; the Third, before or after Mass, at all events before dinner; the Fourth, about the time of Vespers; the Fifth, an hour before supper.

This is more or less the arrangement of hours that I take for granted is being observed in all four Weeks. But as age, condition of health, and the physical constitution of the exercitant permit, there may be five exercises or fewer.

73. ADDITIONAL DIRECTIONS

The purpose of these directions is to help one to go through the exercises better and find more readily what he desires

1. After retiring, just before falling asleep, for the space of a *Hail Mary*, I will think of the hour when I have to rise, and why I am rising, and briefly sum up the exercise I have to go through.

74. 2. When I wake up, I will not permit my thoughts to roam at random, but will turn my mind at once to the subject I

am about to contemplate in the first exercise at midnight. I will seek to rouse myself to shame for my many sins by using examples, let us say, of a knight brought before his king and the whole court, filled with shame and confusion for having grievously offended his lord from whom he had formerly received many gifts and favors. Similarly, in the Second Exercise, I will consider myself a great sinner, loaded with chains, that is, I will look upon myself as bound with fetters, going to appear before the supreme and eternal Judge, and I will recall the way prisoners, bound and deserving of death, appear before an earthly judge. As I dress, I will think over these thoughts or others in keeping with the subject matter of the meditation.

75. 3. I will stand for the space of an *Our Father*, a step or two before the place where I am to meditate or contemplate, and with my mind raised on high, consider that God our Lord beholds me, etc. Then I will make an act of reverence or humility.

76. 4. I will enter upon the meditation, now kneeling, now prostrate upon the ground, now lying face upwards, now seated, now standing, always being intent on seeking what I desire. Hence, two things should be noted:

1. If I find what I desire while kneeling, I will not seek to change my position: if prostrate, I will observe the same direction, etc.
2. I will remain quietly meditating upon the point in which I have found what I desire, without any eagerness to go on till I have been satisfied.

77. 5. After an exercise is finished, either sitting or walking, I will consider for the space of a quarter of an hour how I succeeded in the meditation or contemplation. If poorly, I will

seek the cause of the failure; and after I have found it, I will be sorry, so that I may do better in the future. If I have succeeded, I will give thanks to God our Lord, and the next time try to follow the same method.

78. 6. I should not think of things that give pleasure and joy, as the glory of heaven, the Resurrection, etc., for if I wish to feel pain, sorrow, and tears for my sins, every consideration promoting joy and happiness will impede it. I should rather keep in mind that I want to be sorry and feel pain. Hence it would be better to call to mind death and judgment.

79. 7. For the same reason I should deprive myself of all light, closing the shutters and doors when I am in my room, except when I need light to say prayers, to read, or to eat.

80. 8. I should not laugh or say anything that would cause laughter.

81. 9. I should restrain my eyes except to look up in receiving or dismissing one with whom I have to speak.

PENANCE

82. 10. The tenth Additional Direction deals with penance. This is divided into interior and exterior penance. Interior penance consists in sorrow for one's sins and a firm purpose not to commit them or any others. Exterior penance is the fruit of the first kind. It consists in inflicting punishment on ourselves for the sins we have committed. The principal ways of doing this are three:

83. 1. The first kind of exterior penance concerns eating. In this matter, if we do away with what is superfluous, it is not penance, but temperance. We do penance when we deny ourselves

something of what is suitable for us. The more we do this, the better the penance, provided only we do no harm to ourselves and do not cause any serious illness.

84. 2. The second kind of exterior penance concerns sleep. Here, too, it is not penance when we do away with the superfluous in what is pampering and soft. But it is penance when in our manner of sleeping we take something away from what is suitable. The more we do in this line, the better it is, provided we do not cause any harm to ourselves, and do not bring on any notable illness. But we should not deny ourselves a suitable amount of sleep, except to come to a happy mean in case we had the habit of sleeping too much.

85. 3. The third kind of penance is to chastise the body, that is, to inflict sensible pain on it. This is done by wearing hair shirts, cords, or iron chains on the body, or by scourging or wounding oneself, and by other kinds of austerities.

86. THE MORE SUITABLE AND SAFE FORM OF PENANCE SEEMS TO BE that which would cause sensible pain to the body and not penetrate to the bones, so that it inflicts pain, but does not cause sickness. For this reason, it would seem more suitable to chastise oneself with light cords that cause superficial pain, rather than in any other way that might bring about a serious internal infirmity.

NOTES

87. NOTE I. The principal reason for performing exterior penance is to secure three effects:

1. To make satisfaction for past sins;
2. To overcome oneself, that is, to make our sensual

nature obey reason, and to bring all of our lower facul-
ties into greater subjection to the higher;

3. To obtain some grace or gift that one earnestly desires.
   Thus it may be that one wants a deep sorrow for sin,
   or tears, either because of his sins or because of the
   pains and sufferings of Christ our Lord; or he may
   want the solution of some doubt that is in his mind.

88. NOTE II. Note that the first and second Additional Directions are to be observed for the exercises at midnight and at
daybreak, and not for the exercises made at other times. The
fourth Direction is never to be followed in the church before
others, but only in private, for example, at home.

89. NOTE III. When the exercitant has not found what he has
been seeking, for example, tears, consolation, etc., it is often
useful to make some change in the kind of penance, such as
in food, in sleep, or in other ways of doing penance, so that
we alternate, for two or three days doing penance, and for
two or three not doing any. The reason for this is that more
penance is better for some and less for others. Another reason is that we often quit doing penance because we are too
much concerned about our bodies and erroneously judge that
human nature cannot bear it without notable illness. On the
other hand, at times we may do too much penance, thinking
that the body can stand it. Now since God our Lord knows
our nature infinitely better, when we make changes of this
kind, He often grants each one the grace to understand what
is suitable for him.

90. NOTE IV. The Particular Examination of Conscience will
be made to remove faults and negligences with regard to the
Exercises and the Additional Directions. This will also be
observed in the Second, Third, and Fourth Week.

WHAT IS THE GRACE OF THE FIRST WEEK OF THE SPIRITUAL EXERCISES?

What is the movement...the experience...the gift...the "work" of the First Week of the Spiritual Exercises?

- Read paragraph 53, the colloquy of the First Week, and paragraph 54.

  - This is what sin costs.
  - The love of Christ on the cross is deeper than the damage of sin.
  - With the strength of Christ on the cross, I can look at myself and sin in the world.

- Specificity of love is Christ on the cross. His presence on the cross is love.

  - Shame arises because Christ deserves so much better.
  - Tears are wept when we feel loved and shame at ignoring Christ's love in our own lives.
  - The love of Christ will survive the damage.
  - I'm not alone...abandoned...Christ is with me.
  - Hope arises from being loved by Jesus on the cross.
  - Before Christ on the cross I experience shame and confusion that I'm loved as a sinner (see paragraph 48).
  - The shame not at my being, but at my sins and what I did.
  - Herein is the First Week Act of the Presence of God.

- The grace of the First Week of the Spiritual Exercises:

  - I see the magnanimity of Christ on the cross and I see my own lack of generosity; eyes on Christ on the cross—a consciousness that comes as a product of seeing Christ on the cross.

- ◆ So, Christ on the cross is the ambience, context, image, presence of the First Exercise of the First Week. This must be the context of every meditation and every spiritual exercise of the First Week.
- ◆ The grace must be ministered to the retreatants by Christ…not by my judgment about myself from me… the judgment must come from Christ.

- What is God's view of my sinfulness?

  - ◆ There is a profound realization that I need a Savior… awe and a sense of humility that I need a Savior.
  - ◆ I'm given another opportunity by Christ to follow Him.
  - ◆ A sense of wonder arises and a question: How could this be?
  - ◆ Ignatius does not want hopelessness at sin within retreatants.
  - ◆ There is a feeling of not being afraid to look at and experience evil in the world and in oneself. This lack of fear is a grace—because Christ is with you? A possibility arises.

- Sin destroys the plan of the First Principle and Foundation…Christ restores it.

  - ◆ Embarrassment, shame, and confusion here are in the Ignatian sense.
  - ◆ Yes, I know myself, but Christ says, "I know you more and deeper. My judgment of you is more beautiful and loving than yours is of yourself."
  - ◆ Paragraphs 53 and 54 describe a personal relationship with God…that God can touch a person directly and that a person can talk directly to God.
  - ◆ In Ignatius's time, the Inquisition had a hard time with this, and St. Ignatius was thrown into jail three times for saying, "God talks to you."

- ◆ A balance arises between a sense of God's love for me and a sense of my sin.
- ◆ Sin is so hard to look at that I need only Christ, because only Christ can reveal the depth of sin in the world to me and the depth of my own sin to myself.

I am a loved creation

Despite my sins, I am called to be with God's most loved creation, Jesus Christ. This is the grace of the First Week, the movement of the First Week, and this grace must find a HOME in the retreatant—a home: a place within the retreatant. This is the "WORK" OF THE FIRST WEEK...THE GRACE...THE MOVEMENT of the First Week. So when do I know the retreatant has the gift of the First Week? When they see their history in a uniquely different way. There is a healing in one's history. An event is not gone, it is simply seen in a uniquely different way. Change has begun when "my story"—that is, a retreatant's story—is seen differently. Then there is a healing. The retreatant sees it through the eyes of Christ on the cross. This is an ongoing grace, and when this happens, the "work"...the movement...the gift...the grace of the First Week has been given.

Negative experiences, such as negative authority experiences, sexual experiences, and negative relationships, as well as depression, can block this First Week grace because human beings have a vested interest in mistaken identity; or positive realities in these areas can open up this grace in a retreatant.

SIN is not only what we do or don't do. It is what is done or not done to us, or what should have been done to the retreatant and was not done to the retreatant.

Retreatants are invited to recognize and own that they are a loved creation—man or woman—and are called *because* of their sinfulness and *despite* their sinfulness to accompany the Spirit of God's greatest love.

What are the signs within the experience of the retreatants that say they are asking for and ready for and want the grace of the First Week?

- When retreatants realize they are loved, because the First Week grace is a sense of being loved by Christ on the cross.
- The First Principle and Foundation has brought peace, courage, generosity—a good positive response.
- After having a sense of being loved by God, retreatants can get depressed as a result of realizing they have done this or that evil.
- Somehow retreatants bring up the problem of evil.

The First Exercise: Sin in the world

Shame and confusion have to do with knowing how many have been lost on account of serious sin and how the retreatant has participated in this history of sin in the world.

- The retreatants say I want to accept the First Principle and Foundation, but I don't—and I can't, because I'm not free enough.
- The retreatants feel a need to go back and see what happened in their life—the good and the bad.
- The retreatants want more and say, "God loves me, but I'm restless. There is a dissonance and I don't know why."
- Retreatants realize that there has been a lot of sin in their life and they are not afraid to look at it…at evil…at sin in their personal life.
- The retreatants are wallowing in sin and sinfulness. "I can't get out of it, can't get free of it…I'm stuck…what evil is being done to me?"
- The retreatants are sensing that something is getting in their way, yet they don't know what it is.

- The retreatants sense they are powerless over sin.
- The retreatants are not grateful for God's love.
- Adam and Eve…Cain and Abel…Babel…look at how it spread!
- Self-image emerges as a bad one.

Therefore, the First Week is an explanation to retreatants of what God is already doing in them, because their experience is real but vague. Do not hold a person back. So, you are not directing the retreatants…they are directing you…their experience of God is directing you, the director.

The Second Exercise: One's own sinfulness

- A retreatant says, "I'm in the middle of this history of evil."
- What I see "out there" is "in me."
- I'm involved in "this evil."
- What is "out there" is "in here"…in me.
- I'm part of this evil.
- How can I watch the nightly news and see evil out there and not say that evil is in here, in me?
- Get a mirror. Hold it up…you hypocrite…you finger pointer…that person out there is me.

The Third Exercise: Disordered affections

This takes in disordered motivation—motivation and behavior—and personal responsibility, which are roots of sin. And the roots of sin are different from person to person.

Repetition is necessary to see the deeper knowledge of the disordered affection in me. Disordered affection is a deeper knowledge of the disorder in me. I'm steamrolled by my disorder. Here is the first time the Triple Colloquy is used because of the effect of dealing with disordered affection (paragraph 63). This is difficult and tough. "But for the grace of God go I."

Grace of this Exercise: "There is a false self in me. There is a sinful self in me."

The Fourth Exercise: Repetition of the Third, with the intellect (paragraph 64)

- Find the repetitive pattern of ingrained bad habits by reflecting on the Third Exercise.
- If you give the intellect free range, the intellect looks for consistency and pattern—a habit of behavior and thinking and feeling. Our intellect is seeking "the integrating principle" of our disordered affection.
- This is probably the most powerful and the most important exercise of the First Week.
- The bad habit is deep, and retreatants can feel it hanging over their heads.
- Retreatants "see" the impossibility of stopping themselves: "I'm addicted; it is slavery." "I'm a slave," and "I need a Savior."
- Retreatants "see" a pattern of "failing over and over again," and are realizing they are out of control. The retreatants need the Triple Colloquy.

The grace is bringing to consciousness from the unconscious this pattern of one's own historicity: the history of what one's disordered affection has done to the retreatant.

- You may find Romans 7:14–25 helpful.
- The Fourth Exercise is a SUMMARY and a SYNTHESIS.

The Fifth Exercise: Hell, an application of the senses

- SENTIR: means "to sense" (translated from Spanish; paragraphs 65–71).

- ◆ Retreatants look at their own sin alone—without Christ—tasting of what the full weight of condemnation is like.
- ◆ This isolation is a living death.
- ◆ Imagine yourself having to leave Jesus.
- ◆ Imagine yourself in touch with loss in your life, such as of a loved one, and therefore…the loss of Jesus.
- ◆ Imagine Peter leaving Jesus: "Leave me, Lord, for I'm a sinful man."
- ◆ Imagine your greatest fears are realized, of being abandoned…alone: this is a "hell."
- ◆ Hell is the shame and confusion you have had from yourself, a bad self-image.
- ◆ Imagine yourself being alone with the evil in your life or the evil being done to you.
- ◆ The grace is retreatants realizing that if they continue the way they are going, they are going to go to "hell." Hell could be the outcome.
- ◆ Hell is the extreme of what sin is and does—it takes one away from God. This meditation also gives a heightened awareness of what God has given to the retreatant.

- Hell has been a real red-herring issue. Not to do this meditation has been the norm, when actually it is an application of the senses and prayer, and doing it would better serve the retreatant.

  - ◆ Retreatants begin to realize they are still free to reject God's love.
  - ◆ Hell is if sin becomes the controlling element in the retreatant's life.
  - ◆ This is psychologically intensifying.
  - ◆ The question is, What takes me away from God?

- What is the progression here? Go over the meaning and graces of the five exercises of the First Week.

- Why is the First Exercise first? Why is the Second, second? The Third, third? The Fourth, fourth? The Fifth, fifth?
- The direction is from the outer reality to one's inner real self.
- It is safer to start "outside" of oneself with an "objective" look at sin outside of oneself first then within oneself. This is a sort of finger-pointing exercise.
- There is a sense of security starting in the "outside" first, and doing this we gain a sense of security as we proceed.
- The realization is a movement to a personal appropriation of sin.

HOW DOES ST. IGNATIUS GIVE THE FIRST WEEK? (PARAGRAPH 72)

As the retreat progresses: Reread the Act of the Presence of God and ask, How did it go?

Remember that spiritual direction is to afford two qualities: freedom and encouragement. Refer to St. John of the Cross in *The Living Flame of Love* (paragraphs 27–63). Initially I spoke of an allergic reaction in the direction to a retreatant. Now I want to bring up the opposite reaction—the reaction of love: a love reaction. You should expect retreatants to love you. And you should expect that you will love them. We can't help that. They can't help that. And there are emotional overtones and undertones to that love.

As a director, do you have an allergic reaction to your love for your retreatants? How do you give the first exercise of the First Week of the Spiritual Exercises? This is a week of LOVE…YES…and so the two questions remain: What did God say to you? and How do you feel?

The director is not to rescue retreatants from the pain of evil

Where should this go? Have the retreatant read today's newspaper.

How do you handle the retreatant's self-image? A bad self-image is an old-fashioned word for repressed hurt, anger, need, and sorrow. Retreatants may not be able to go to their own insides for information because they are afraid of what is there. They say they can't handle any evil at all, or any consideration of evil—they say they can only handle positive feelings of love and joy.

The Act of the Presence of God during the First Week: "I am beheld." It is Christ beholding me from the cross: this is really a contemplation in the Ignatian sense. This ensures that the *experience* of the retreat is primary by establishing a clear idea of what St. Ignatius means.

An Act of the Presence of God: What is it? What is it not? (75:3). Make a point of bringing it up.

Confidentiality: this is a time where you can take the time to bring up an experience you or your retreatant is having.

Chapter 3

THE PROGRESSION WITHIN THE EXERCISES OF THE FIRST WEEK

A PRE-NOTE

St. John of the Cross says we would be very surprised to know how fast God wants a person to progress in the spiritual life. The major problem is bad spiritual direction and temptation, and lack of intelligence. John talks about bad spiritual direction as a spiritual director forcing a directee to go through the exact same experience or regimentation as the director himself or herself went through and experienced, and not allowing the directee to simply be with God. John talks about the pain experienced from bad spiritual direction in *Living Flame of Love* (paragraphs 27–63).

It is very important, therefore, to move a person as soon as the signs are there that they are ready for the next exercise. For example, I directed a young priest from Alaska who, after seven days, had finished the entire First and Second Weeks. He had received the graces of the First and Second Weeks. I moved him as fast as he received the graces of each exercise. I was anxious, nervous, and fearful because we had three weeks to go and he was entering the Third Week of the exercises. I trusted God and I trusted this young priest's experience. In the next three weeks, he was in the Third Week and was called by Christ to start a new religious order in Magadan in Siberia, Russia, which he did.

For a retreatant to progress appropriately,

- Do all of the First Week before Christ on the cross—this is really a contemplation—an Act of the Presence of God.
- Sin described by Nathan to David is easy to see in a third party: 2 Samuel 12:1–13.
- Inordinate affection at its base is good affection. The seven capital sins come from good affections that have become disordered.
- The First Exercise addresses how good affections become disordered.

HOW DO YOU GIVE THE FIRST EXERCISE?

This is A WEEK OF LOVE—the love of Christ on the cross… really a contemplation, not a meditation. We directors must not try to rescue the retreatants from the pain and power of evil in the world and in themselves through their lives and history. You will help them face evil in themselves without allowing their own bad self-image to take over and cause them to be unable to accept it.

What do you do?

- The Act of the Presence of God: Christ beholding the retreatant from the cross.
- Read the autobiography of St. Ignatius of Loyola, where he describes unexplained desolation.

Image of self—image of God and the Exercises of the First Week

The Examination of Conscience, personal sin, confession, and rules for the discernment of spirits:

How does this all work together in the First Week?

- Romans 1:18–32, *God has left humanity to its own sinfulness*
- Genesis 3:1–24, *the fall of Adam and Eve*
- Psalms 50:1–23, *worship in Spirit and truth*
- Psalms 106, *a national confusion*
- Psalms 107, *God is a refuge in all dangers*
- Hosea 2:4–25, *God and his unfaithful wife*
- Ezekiel 16, *an allegorical history of Israel*
- Hosea 11:1–11, *God's love despised*
- Revelation 12:7, *angels fight the satanic spirits*
- Genesis 1—11, *from creation until Abraham's call*
- Genesis 6, *grief of God seeing the world of sin*
- Romans 1:18–25, *God's anger against pagans*

  - ◆ Sin: Polluted atmosphere you have to breathe, and all is exacerbated.
  - ◆ Sin is the very air we breathe. Calcutta was 126 degrees in April 2018.
  - ◆ It is shocking. We are in prison. We live in prison.

- Luke 5:8, *Peter says, "Depart from me."*
- Luke 15:11–32, *the prodigal son*
- Luke 18:13, *tax collectors and sinners*

How do you give the Second Exercise?

- The retreatants recall behavior, actions, and performance… sin.

- Make an inventory…by years…by jobs…by places one lived…or in other ways.
- Peter weeping.
- The women weeping.
- Look at the times I loved and was loved, was hurt and hurt others, both intentionally and unintentionally.
- Remembering, with a prayer of reminiscence.
- Where does the view of myself come from? It must come from Christ on the cross.
- Reflect on applicable Scriptures:

  - Ezekiel 37, *the dry bones*
  - Psalm 38:1–23, *prayer in distress*
  - Psalm 32, *candid admission of sin*
  - Psalm 51, *Miserere*
  - 1 John 1:5—2:2, *walk in the light*
  - Romans 7:14–25, *the inward struggle*
  - Romans 8:19–23, *glory as our destiny*
  - Galatians 5:13–22, *liberty and love*
  - 2 Samuel 12:1–12, *Nathan and David*
  - Luke 15, *lost and found parables*
  - 2 Peter 2, *graphic sins of individuals*

- Read David Hassel, SJ's, book *Radical Prayer*: remembering times people loved you and times you loved other people; times people hurt you and times you hurt other people; times you sinned and times you were sinned against.
- This is like St. Ignatius saying, "Go back over the years and places where you lived your life…look back."

How do you give the Third Exercise?

I suggest giving it a full day for the retreatant to obtain a deeper knowledge of the disordered affection:

- "I'm steamrolled by my disorder."

- Here for the first time, the Triple Colloquy is used, because of the effect of my dealing with disordered affection.
- Ask retreatants to look at and reread their retreat notes of the last days and see the CONSOLATIONS and DESO-LATIONS, or anything else that is significant.

  ◆ Looking back is like sifting sand and rocks looking for gold.
  ◆ Be more careful and gentler about what moves you slightly and subtly.

- Pray the Triple Colloquy asking for the grace of the first and second points of the colloquy, meaning ask Mary to give you the grace and bring you to Jesus, seeking a "feeling knowledge of one's disordered affections" and a deeper knowledge in a feeling way of them.

How do you give the Fourth Exercise?

I would consider giving it a full day.

- Repetition of the Third Exercise with the intellect (paragraph 64).
- Find the repetitive pattern of ingrained bad habits by reflection.
- A reaction could be that the bad habit is deep and "I'm in over my head."
- The Fourth Exercise is seeing the pattern in one's disordered affection—it isn't intellectual reflection on all my disordered affections.
- One would "see" the impossibility of stopping one's self.
- One could see a pattern of "over and over, again and again."
- Grace of the Fourth Exercise is a feeling knowledge of what this has done to me.
- Romans 8:31–39, *a hymn to God's love.*

- How does one stand in the way of God's grace?
- Ask the retreatants to go back over their history. Ask the question, "Is this the first time you have experienced this disordered affection?" We are looking for a pattern.
- The Fourth Exercise is a "summary"—a summing up looking for a pattern of habit, looking for a habit.

  - ◆ This brings up a deep need for God…so here one needs the Triple Colloquy.
  - ◆ Is this an isolated occurrence, this "sin," or is this a habit?
  - ◆ Repeat the Triple Colloquy.

How do you give the Fifth Exercise?

How *long* do you give retreatants this "contemplation"? How many prayer periods? How long do you give a person the prayer on hell?

How to give this prayer?

- Psalms of abandonment—like Psalms 13, 22, 63.
- Imagine no music, no beauty, no talents, and so on. Feel what that would be like.
- Imagine being alone in your struggle against sin and evil.
- Judas pulling away from Jesus…dying by suicide.
- We are made for "limitless love," now imagining if that is lost—how awful that loss would be…and is.
- You have experienced consolation from Christ on the cross talking as one friend to another, as you look at evil and sin in the world and evil and sin in your own life and in your own self. What if you didn't experience that consolation? That is hell.
- We assume that we are going to heaven; it is the fabric of our faith life being, the air we breathe—what if there was no heaven to hope in? That is hell.

- You have looked at the pattern of your "bad habits" of repetitive evil in the past—hell is "the future" of your evil habits, an eternal life of being bound to your sins and evil habits.
- We are made for "limitless love" and if that is lost, the loss is what hell would be.
- Separation is hell.
- Hell is touching into our sense of emptiness.
- One's disordered affection and habit is so powerful, it could take over: that is hell.
- A sense that hell could happen very easily: that is scary and that is hell.
- Without Christ is hell.
- Seven capital sins: pride, envy, lust, greed, gluttony, wrath, and sloth.

Compare Gandhi's seven social sins: Wealth without work; commerce without morality; science without humanity; pleasure without conscience; politics without principles; knowledge without character; and worship without sacrifice.

THE GRACE OF THE FIRST WEEK—THE MOVEMENT...THE EXPERIENCE...THE GIFT... AND THE "WORK" OF THE FIRST WEEK

At this point in the retreat, return to the Act of the Presence of God. And ask, "How is it going?" Remember that spiritual direction is to afford two qualities: freedom and encouragement from St. John of the Cross in *Living Flame of Love*, paragraphs 27–63.

Do you have an allergic reaction to your love for your retreatants?

To negotiate this successfully, you need to check out the quotient of your neediness—your need to be loved—right now; your need to be wanted; and your need to be comforted—right now. Give the example of carrying bags of groceries from the car to the kitchen and there being soccer balls and dolls and footballs and baseball bats in the walkway. If you are aware of them, you will not fall and injure yourself.

What is your need for attention right now?

What is the grace of paragraph 53, the colloquy of the First Week, and of paragraph 54?

The retreatant can see

- This is what sin costs.
- The love of Christ on the cross is deeper than the damage.
- With the strength of Christ on the cross I can look at myself.
- Specificity of love is Christ on the cross.
- Shame because Christ deserves so much better.
- Tears are wept when we feel loved and shame.
- That love will survive the damage.
- I'm not alone…not abandoned.
- Hopeful from being loved by Jesus.
- Before Christ on the cross: there is shame and confusion that I'm loved as a sinner (paragraph 48). This shame is not at my being, but at my sins and what I did.

I see the magnanimity of Christ on the cross and I see my own lack of generosity: eyes on Christ on the cross—a consciousness that comes as a product of seeing Christ on the cross. Christ on the cross is the ambience, context, image, and presence of the First Exercise of the First Week. This must be the context of every meditation and every spiritual exercise of the First Week.

So, the grace must be ministered to me by Christ and not through my judgment about myself from me: the judgment must come from Christ.

This entails

- God's view of my sinfulness.
- Profound realization that I need a Savior—awe—and a sense of humility that I need a Savior.
- I'm given another opportunity.
- A sense of wonder. A contrast: How could this be?
- Ignatius does not want hopelessness at sin within a retreatant.
- Not being afraid to look at and experience evil in the world and in oneself. This lack of fear is a grace because Christ is with the retreatant.
- Sin destroys the plan of the First Principle and Foundation.
- Yes, I know myself: Christ says I know you more and deeper. My judgment of you is more beautiful and loving than yours is of yourself.

I am invited to recognize and own that I am a loved creation—man or woman—called because of my sinfulness (and despite my sinfulness) to accompany the Spirit of God's greatest love, Jesus. What are the signs within the experience of the retreatants that say that they are asking for and are ready for and want the grace of the First Week?

- When retreatants realize they are loved, because First Week grace is a sense of being loved by Christ on the cross.
- The First Principle and Foundation has brought peace, courageousness, generosity—a good positive response.
- After a sense of being loved by God, they get depressed as a result that they have done this or that evil.
- Somehow, they bring up the problem of evil.
- I want to accept the First Principle and Foundation, but I don't—and I can't because I'm not free enough.
- I need to go back and see what happened in my life, good and bad.

- I want more: God loves me, but I'm restless and I don't know why.
- There has been a lot of sin in my life, but I'm not afraid... to look at it...at evil...at sin in my personal life.
- I'm wallowing in my sin—*my* sinfulness.
- Something is getting in my way and I don't know what it is.
- I'm powerless over sin.
- I'm not grateful for God's Love.
- Adam and Eve...Cain and Abel...Babel...look how it spread.

The First Week, therefore, is an explanation to retreatants of what God is already doing in them, because their experience is real but vague.

Chapter 4

THE EXAMINATION OF CONSCIENCE

THE ART OF DIRECTING THE EXERCISES

Pre-Note 1

Five persons are involved in the spiritual direction within the context of the Spiritual Exercises:

1. The director
2. The retreatant
3. God, our Creator and Lord
4. St. Ignatius
5. Satan

Balancing these five is the art of directing the Spiritual Exercises.

Pre-Note 2

A director may need to see a retreatant twice a day during these days of the First Week.

Pre-Note 3

Like Christ, a director takes on the brokenness, darkness, desolation, and depravity of those we serve. This is an earmark of the ministry of Christ. So, a director experiences the same sin and evil as the retreatant experiences: a darkness, a "heaviness," a depression, and a desolation. Welcome it. Yes, welcome it. Bring it in. Experience it. Suffer it.

An impatience—an oversensitivity—an irritability...a vague painful restlessness...or an UNDERSENSITIVITY...OR INSENSITIVITY...A NUMBNESS that covers the pain in a director? The hymn of Philippians 2:7 is the methodology of Christ saving us: Christ emptied Himself, becoming one of us—assuming the condition of human beings...and saved us.

Pre-Note 4

- A bad self-image. What is it?
- What is a bad image of God? A projected bad self-image. It is a transference of hurt, anger, pain, sorrow, and need, which is unprocessed in a retreatant.
- God: One who expects you to be worthy before you can receive grace—a God who is a tyrant—a punishing God, not to be trusted—a God who is disappointed with me, vengeful, distant, making God in my own image.
- What is a bad image of the Church?

How do you give the First Week to a person who has a bad self-image, a bad image of God, and a bad image of the Church?

Move them into the Second Week material in contemplation, asking for the grace: Let me see, O Lord, that You are doing this for me...always for me! This is the gift of the First Week. Often, in the

Third Week, this First Week gift is given…like the colloquy of the First Week before Christ on the cross, paragraph 53.

Have the retreatants go back to their experience of being loved, any experience of being loved they have had. Have them go over this experience…or all of the experiences they have of being loved. If they feel they have never felt that they have been loved, have them make a list of what was good in their lives. What experience or experiences of joy have there ever been in your life?

Then have them

- Make an inventory of love experiences.
- Make an inventory of good things that have happened in their life.

An emerging problem will have contours. What are the contours in the retreatant? God is often the origin of the problem, and God forces it up.

An exercise that would apply here is to imagine being alone in your struggle against sin!

THE EXAMINATION OF CONSCIENCE (PARAGRAPH 43)

Pre-Note 1

St. Ignatius considered the most important prayer of the Spiritual Exercises to be the Examination of Conscience.

Pre-Note 2

St. Ignatius told the early Jesuits that if they cannot celebrate Eucharist, or do an hour of prayer, they must do their Examination of Conscience twice a day.

Pre-Note 3

I developed three torn discs; how did it happen? I decided to do something good for myself by jogging each day for twenty minutes and doing the 5BX exercise program of the Royal Canadian Mounted Police that I learned in college. I did this six days a week for seven years. One day, while doing these exercises at the beach, I was unable to move, unable to stand up straight. To the hospital and then to sports orthopedic and rehabilitation at Stanford I went. "What happened to you?" the doctor asked. When I told him, he said that every time I did those exercises, I injured my back. "You mean I did this to myself, Doctor?" He said, "Yes, you did this to yourself... trying to do something good for yourself, you did something bad for yourself."

Sincerity is the least of the virtues!

Learning to do this Exercise correctly

Learning to do this exercise correctly is a must, as with my experience of doing physical therapy. You must teach it correctly and check that it is done correctly, like going back to school for eight and a half months to have the physical therapist look at how you are doing the exercises. All the physical therapist did was just teach me to do the exercises correctly—no massage. Such is the importance of this spiritual direction work.

- This is a Spiritual Exercise.
- This is a method of prayer.
- This is a charismatic gift of prayer of Ignatius.

This Spiritual Exercise is to develop the gift of "seeing God in all things." The Examination of Conscience is like tuning a violin string to keep the instrument in tune with itself and with the orchestra—or tuning any instrument. It is the correcting of a compass, as if you are off one degree; you will be far off course soon if it is not adjusted. The Examination of Conscience is a touchstone for all of the Spiritual Exercises of the spiritual life.

There are many spiritual exercises of St. Ignatius, including meditations, contemplations, the Examination of Conscience, vocal prayers, considerations, the Act of the Presence of God. ONLY TWO are important enough to be embedded in the retreatants' being when they complete the spiritual exercises and leave in thirty days: the Examination of Conscience and the Act of the Presence of God.

The five basic features and dimensions of the Examination of Conscience:

1. THE ACT OF THE PRESENCE OF GOD: Psalm 139

- Not as I would have it that I behold God, but that God is beholding me now, and God is seeing me, now.
- Take one minute on this.

2. A PETITION TO SEE GOD IN MY DAY

- This is a fairness prayer—a prayer of reciprocity.
- "If You see me, O God, let me see You in my day today."
- Take about one minute on this.

3. REFLECTIVE OVERVIEW OF THE LAST PORTION OF MY DAY, LOOKING FOR GOD'S PRESENSE AND MOVEMENTS

- Go over and view the videotape of my day: let it run, but give God the clicker...give God time to show you God's Self in your day.
- Let God freeze-frame the tape and show you God's Self.
- Take about four to five minutes on this.

4. MY REACTIONS TO THIS

- I may give applause for what God did and where God was; I may experience some healing sorrow at what I did (perhaps).
- Take one minute.

5. LOOK AHEAD AT THE NEXT PORTION OF MY DAY WITH THIS RENEWED SENSITIVITY

- "Oh, yes, I have a meeting with that same person whom I smashed this afternoon."
- With a fresh grace, I can live as Christ lived.
- This should take one minute.

This entire prayer should take ten to twelve minutes Like all other prayers, stop and be fed where God feeds you. It is not important to finish each dimension each time as "homework," but rather just give God time, and go with your Creator and Lord.

How do you know retreatants are asking for the Examination of Conscience?

- When they are looking at their own life…their own history.
- "I can't interpret the movements of my own life: joy, love, sorrow, fear, pain—and emerging problems."
- "I would like to have a more affective emotional life. I live in my head."
- "How do I find God? I have a lot of distractions."
- "How do I know God's will?"
- "How do I know my deepest feelings?"
- "How do I keep in touch with my experience?"
- When a retreatant is having spiritual experiences outside of prayer and says,

- ◆ "How do I track them? How do I see them, notice them, not waste them, appreciate them, hold on to them, relish them, receive them, receive the grace and not miss it?"
- ◆ This is accomplished by developing the grace…the sensitivity…the skill of the Examination of Conscience prayer.

- "Is it God? Is it God's Grace?"
- They are already doing Examination of Conscience in an intuitive way, saying in effect, "I need to see God better to be more aware of God's movement."
- They are showing and expressing a need to take stock of their lives.
- They go to bed depressed from their day. Give the Examination of Conscience as a way for them to see there was something good that happened in their day. Ask, Where did that come from?
- Ask the retreatants how they feel and they don't know. "No one ever asked me that before."
- Developing the sensitivity to receive and catch the unexpected—the surprise—presence of God on the run.
- To help them notice what they are noticing.
- "I wish I could always be aware of God, as I am aware of God on this retreat."
- "I want to put order in my life."
- "I want to summarize my life."
- "I have a devotion to the Holy Spirit and I want to see the Holy Spirit in my day more somehow."
- "I want to become more sensitive to God and to God's Presence—I'm so insensitive."
- "My spiritual life is compartmentalized. I pray in the morning and it seems that prayer is not part of the rest of the day, throughout the day."
- "I'd like to be more reflective."

The Examination of Conscience is a way to help them "pay attention" to what is going on.

Giving the Examination of Conscience

- The Examination of Conscience establishes humility by practicing it.
- The Examination of Conscience is like putting your hand in a stream and feeling the flow and temperature of the water twice a day.
- Recommended reading: *The Life of Saint Ignatius, Experiencing God in Daily Life.*

Chapter 5

THE RULES FOR THE DISCERNMENT OF SPIRITS OF THE FIRST WEEK OF THE SPIRITUAL EXERCISES

From the text of the Spiritual Exercises of St. Ignatius of Loyola:

313. RULES FOR THE DISCERNMENT OF SPIRITS

I

Rules for understanding to some extent the different movements produced in the soul and for recognizing those that are good to admit them, and those that are bad, to reject them. These rules are more suited to the first week

314. 1. In the case of those who go from one mortal sin to another, the enemy is ordinarily accustomed to propose apparent pleasures. He fills their imagination with sensual delights and gratifications, the more readily to keep them in their vices and increase the number of their sins.

With such persons the good spirit uses a method which is the reverse of the above. Making use of the light of reason, he will rouse the sting of conscience and fill them with remorse.

315. 2. In the case of those who go on earnestly striving to cleanse their souls from sin and who seek to rise in the service of God our Lord to greater perfection, the method pursued is the opposite of that mentioned in the first rule.

Then it is characteristic of the evil spirit to harass with anxiety, to afflict with sadness, to raise obstacles backed by fallacious reasonings that disturb the soul. Thus he seeks to prevent the soul from advancing.

It is characteristic of the good spirit, however, to give courage and strength, consolations, tears, inspirations, and peace. This He does by making all easy, by removing all obstacles so that the soul goes forward in doing good.

316. 3. Spiritual Consolation. I call it consolation when an interior movement is aroused in the soul, by which it is inflamed with love of its Creator and Lord, and as a consequence, can love no creature on the face of the earth for its own sake, but only in the Creator of them all. It is likewise consolation when one sheds tears that move to the love of God, whether it be because of sorrow for sins, or because of the sufferings of Christ our Lord, or for any other reason that is immediately directed to the praise and service of God. Finally, I call consolation every increase of faith, hope, and love, and all interior joy that invites and attracts to what is heavenly and to the salvation of one's soul by filling it with peace and quiet in its Creator and Lord.

317. 4. Spiritual Desolation. I call desolation what is entirely the opposite of what is described in the third rule, as darkness of

soul, turmoil of spirit, inclination to what is low and earthly, restlessness rising from many disturbances and temptations which lead to want of faith, want of hope, want of love. The soul is wholly slothful, tepid, sad, and separated, as it were, from its Creator and Lord. For just as consolation is the opposite of desolation, so the thoughts that spring from consolation are the opposite of those that spring from desolation.

318. 5. In time of desolation, we should never make any change, but remain firm and constant in the resolution and decision which guided us the day before the desolation, or in the decision to which we adhered in the preceding consolation. For just as in consolation the good spirit guides and counsels us, so in desolation the evil spirit guides and counsels. Following his counsels, we can never find the way to a right decision.

319. 6. Though in desolation we must never change our former resolutions, it will be very advantageous to intensify our activity against the desolation. We can insist more upon prayer, upon meditation, and on much examination of ourselves. We can make an effort in a suitable way to do some penance.

320. 7. When one is in desolation, he should be mindful that God has left him to his natural powers to resist the different agitations and temptations of the enemy in order to try him. He can resist with the help of God, which always remains, though he may not clearly perceive it. For though God has taken from him the abundance of fervor and overflowing love and the intensity of His favors, nevertheless, he has sufficient grace for eternal salvation.

321. 8. When one is in desolation, he should strive to persevere in patience. This reacts against the vexations that have overtaken him. Let him consider, too, that consolation will soon

return, and in the meantime, he must diligently use the means against desolation which have been given in the sixth rule.

322. 9. The principal reasons why we suffer from desolation are three:

The first is because we have been tepid and slothful or negligent in our exercises of piety, and so through our own fault spiritual consolation has been taken away from us.

The second reason is because God wishes to try us, to see how much we are worth, and how much we will advance in His service and praise when left without the generous reward of consolations and signal favors.

The third reason is because God wishes to give us a true knowledge and understanding of ourselves, so that we may have an intimate perception of the fact that it is not within our power to acquire and attain great devotion, intense love, tears, or any other spiritual consolation; but that all this is the gift and grace of God our Lord. God does not wish us to build on the property of another, to rise up in spirit in a certain pride and vainglory and attribute to ourselves the devotion and other effects of spiritual consolation.

323. 10. When one enjoys consolation, let him consider how he will conduct himself during the time of ensuing desolation, and store up a supply of strength as defense against that day.

324. 11. He who enjoys consolation should take care to humble himself and lower himself as much as possible. Let him recall how little he is able to do in time of desolation, when he is left without such grace or consolation.

On the other hand, one who suffers desolation should remember that by making use of the sufficient grace offered him, he can do much to withstand all his enemies. Let him find his strength in his Creator and Lord.

325. 12. The enemy conducts himself as a weakling before a show of strength, and a tyrant if he has his will. It is characteristic of the enemy in a quarrel with a man to lose courage and take to flight if the man shows that he is determined and fearless. However, if the man loses courage and begins to flee, the anger, vindictiveness, and rage of the enemy surge up and know no bounds. In the same way, the enemy becomes weak, loses courage, and turns to flight with his seductions as soon as one leading a spiritual life faces his temptations boldly, and does exactly the opposite of what he suggests. However, if one begins to be afraid and to lose courage in temptations, no wild animal on earth can be more fierce than the enemy of our human nature. He will carry out his perverse intentions with consummate malice.

326. 13. Our enemy may also be compared in his manner of acting to a false lover. He seeks to remain hidden and does not want to be discovered. If such a lover speaks with evil intention to the daughter of a good father, or to the wife of a good husband, and seeks to seduce them, he wants his words and solicitations kept secret. He is greatly displeased if his evil suggestions and depraved intentions are revealed by the daughter to her father, or by the wife to her husband. Then he readily sees he will not succeed in what he has begun. In the same way, when the enemy of our human nature tempts a just soul with his wiles and seductions, he earnestly desires that they be received secretly and kept secret. But if one manifests them to a confessor, or to some other spiritual person who understands his deceits and malicious designs, the evil one is very much vexed. For he knows that he cannot succeed in his evil undertaking once his evident deceits have been revealed.

327. 14. The conduct of our enemy may also be compared to the tactics of a leader intent upon seizing and plundering a

position he desires. A commander and leader of an army will encamp, explore the fortifications and defenses of the stronghold, and attack at the weakest point. In the same way, the enemy of our human nature investigates from every side all our virtues, theological, cardinal, and moral. Where he finds the defenses of eternal salvation weakest and most deficient, there he attacks and tries to take us by storm.

RULES FOR DISCERNMENT OF SPIRITS OF THE FIRST WEEK OF THE SPIRITUAL EXERCISES

Paragraph 313

These Rules are a treasure for the Church given to St. Ignatius through the Society of Jesus. I would like to honor their place in the history of ascetical theology by having you READ THEM OUT LOUD slowly as you walk around your own room.

Why are these the Rules of the First Week? Because they deal with gross evil and gross temptations.

Do you believe in the devil?

- The DEVIL: the word comes from *diabolus*, meaning "the divider."
- What about Jesus being tempted on the temple? Or in the desert?
- This is an issue of power—in a name. The reason I believe in a personal devil—Satan—is because in using the name Satan or the devil I have power over it. Using the example of knowing someone's name: when you use it, a deep personal reaction occurs…you get their attention. If I say, "Hey, you," I get a reaction but not the depth of personal attentional energy I get when I use the actual name.

What is the content of these First Week Rules?

The Rules of the First Week address

- The struggle between good and evil: consolations and desolations.
- The struggle between GRACE and SINFULNESS—EVIL.
- The struggle between MOVING TOWARD GOD and MOVING AWAY FROM GOD.
- Facing indifference toward all things and working toward that and with that is a logical follow-up from the First Principle and Foundation.

These rules contain

- Four guidelines for consolation.
- Two guidelines for desolation.

Signs when the retreatants are asking for the Rules for the Discernment of Spirits of the First Week

What are the signs from their experience?

- I have been interfered with by "influences" and they appear to be authentic and real.
- Agitation: if they have been agitated—out of the blue—with power.
- These rules help them make sense out of their movements.
- There is a sorrow of something emerging...so the Rules get them to say what it is: to speak the truth about this movement.
- There is a sense of being confused.
- Deep desolation...to see where it is from and see where it is going.

- Deep consolation…also to see where it is from and where it is going.
- "I don't understand what is going on in me"…to make sense of what is going on in the retreatant.
- "Why do I do what I do?" the retreatant asks.
- A retreatant loses touch with their inner self throughout the day.
- These Rules correct a retreatant's inner climate—the Examination of Conscience brings them back to their center.
- The struggle of their journey begins to arise, and there is a clarification of what is going on within them.
- Looking at their past decisions and the question arises: "Why am I feeling the way I am?"
- There is a sudden "shift" from consolation to desolation—from "grace" to "worry" or some significant disturbances arise.
- A retreatant says, "I don't know if it is God talking to me."
- Nagging doubts begin to arise, and they don't know where they are coming from.
- Confusion about what is going on within begins to arise.
- There is disruptive chaos continuing within a person.

In giving these Rules, it is a very real type of "appeal to authority" as retreatants see, "What is happening to me is codified in these Rules and explaining to me what is inside me now…from a saint who lived and wrote four hundred and fifty years ago." This brings a sense of dignity when they thought their interior experience was aberrant. It brings peace and a confidence "to look within."

Giving the Rules for the Discernment of Spirits

How do you give them and apply them?

- As the retreatants confront their consolations and desolations in themselves in their own experience.

- Read them and direct the retreatants to read a specific rule that will apply to a specific issue or dynamic in their experience now.
- Retreatants say, "God made me do this or that." Ask them, "How do you know that was God?" Then say, "Ignatius has guidelines and rules that could help in finding out and answering this."
- What are you learning about these Rules now?
- What is the interface between the Examination of Conscience and these Rules?
- Do you believe in the devil?

The art of listening

- How do you do the First Week and how do you give the Rules for Discernment of Spirits of the First Week to a person who has a bad self-image?
- How do you give the Rules for Discernment of Spirits of the First Week to a person who has a bad image of God?
- What is the interface between the Examination of Conscience and the Rules for Discernment of Spirits of the First Week?
- What is the organic synergy between the Examination of Conscience and the Rules for the Discernment of Spirits?
- What is "the mood of the day"?
- What is the difference between depression and desolation? Books can and have been written about this. I make some very introductory remarks simply to bring up the differences.

DEPRESSION

- Depression touches all aspects of your life. For example, you can't have fun with your friends as you used to.

- There is no sense of meaning.
- One experiences no joy in the sunshine, in walks, in music.
- A person does not want to pray.
- There is conscious and unconscious anger.
- The rest of your life is not working; there is a paralysis.

DESOLATION

- Desolation touches only one dimension of your life—the spiritual one. You can have fun with your friends… and still be in desolation.
- There is a sense of meaning—in suffering.
- There is a felt knowledge that consolation will return.
- There is joy in the sunshine, in walks, in music.
- There is a sense of being tempted.
- A person wants to pray. The rest of your life is working. You can function. One can pray.

Look at interior and exterior penance, paragraphs 82, 86, and 89; the general examen; sacrament of reconciliation; and midnight meditation.

THE GRACE OF THE SECOND WEEK OF THE SPIRITUAL EXERCISES

What are the signs one is ready for the Second Week? How do you give the Second Week?

During this time in the spiritual exercises, the full thirty days, ask your retreatants if they want another director.

REVIEW

- Examination of Conscience: it is a bit of an insult to our being as it says what I do or don't do is not the center of the world. God is the center of the world—heliocentricity in true cosmology.

- What God is doing is more important than what I'm doing. It teaches humility.
- What am I experiencing now as a person...as a director?
- What is happening in me now?
- How is this making me feel?
- What am I experiencing NOW with my retreatants?
- What are my retreatants experiencing NOW?
- How are my retreatants moving through the First Week?
- What problems am I encountering with my individual retreatants? And how am I resolving them?
- What are the graces you are having in directing your retreatants NOW?
- What are you as a director experiencing NOW about the Spiritual Exercises and about St. Ignatius?

SECOND WEEK

Chapter 6

THE SECOND WEEK OF THE SPIRITUAL EXERCISES

This chapter is about the structure and the meaning of the Second Week of the Spiritual Exercises. In beginning a consideration of the Second Week, let us look at where we have come from during this First Week.

A REVIEW

I experience shame and confusion at being loved by Christ even though I am a sinner: What have I done in return for Christ? What does Christ see in me? Why would Christ love me?

The grace of the First Week: I evaluate myself as guilty, but after looking at Christ on the cross and talking to Him, I evaluate myself as loved—as Christ evaluates me. Are you as a director or retreatant experiencing any new element of the grace of the First Week?

PRE-NOTE

AN EPISTEMOLOGICAL PRINCIPLE: What I am coming to know determines the methodology of how I come to know it.

If you want to know the multiplication tables, you memorize them:

$$2 \times 2 = 4$$

If you want to know a person, you simply be with that person in many varied settings and experiences, such as shopping, dining, working, painting, cleaning, playing sports, going on picnics, and traveling.

The method of coming to know Jesus is the prayer of contemplation.

- Contemplation is different than meditation.
- Contemplation is getting to know a person. Michelangelo lived with the stone in his studio before he carved his David.

WHAT IS THE GIFT OF THE SECOND WEEK OF THE SPIRITUAL EXERCISES?

The gift of Ignatian contemplation: How do you know when you have it?

- You know you have the gift of the Second Week of the Spiritual Exercises when your own life comes up while you are keeping your eyes on Jesus!

  - This is "the now"…"me now"…the specificity of the Kingdom Meditation, calling to me in my day for a specific purpose in the world during my concrete lifetime.
  - This is the specificity of the incarnation NOW—God now looking down on the earth and sending me now… my world…my life…my lifetime; it is a specific call now…a specific job—now!

- What is the relationship between the story of Jesus and my story?
- What is the relationship between the experience of Jesus and my experience?

  - ◆ The structure of Luke–Acts: written by the same person to express what the apostles experienced and lived out, which was exactly the same as what Jesus experienced and lived out…and so, it is the same with me—the same with the retreatant. This means going beyond a head trip and a two thousand-years-ago historical Jesus, and coming to a contemporary reality and dimension.
  - ◆ The Gospel of Matthew is a historical present, with the use in Greek of the present tense for past experience—the call of the disciples in the present tense, writing like Damon Runyon wrote. What Jesus did then, Jesus is doing now…this is also in the agony in the Garden. Jesus asks his disciples to stay and watch with Him.

- A call and a grace for personal participation by retreatants in the mystery of Christ here and now.

  - ◆ How does this happen…in the twenty-first century and in the year 33…in Christ?
  - ◆ The mystery of Christ's life is now always happening. What we thought happened in time is transcending time. What we thought happened in Jesus's lifetime to Jesus two thousand years ago is now happening to retreatants here and now in the retreat two thousand years later.

- Retreatants are and become themselves in the contemplation—their real simple deepest selves.

THE GRACE OF THE SECOND WEEK—THE MOVEMENT...THE EXPERIENCE...THE GIFT... AND THE "WORK" OF THE SECOND WEEK

THE FIRST STEP

What is the grace of the Second Week of the Spiritual Exercises (paragraph 104) according to St. Ignatius?

- An intimate knowledge of the Lord that I may love Him more intimately and follow Him more closely: a personal knowledge and love and familiarity of Christ as a person.
- My call to accompany God in creation is now the call to accompany Jesus in the redemption and fulfillment of creation, the reign of God, now, two thousand years later.

THE SECOND STEP

What are the signs within the experience of the retreatant that they are asking you to give them the Second Week of the spiritual exercises?

Retreatants are ready for the Second Week when they have

- No time parameters for their prayer.
- An ability to spend a long time in prayer on a small detail.
- A desire to know and love the One who is saving them.
- A desire to respond to God's forgiving love.
- An ease and facility with the Triple Colloquy.
- A curiosity about Jesus. A desire to know Jesus.
- An ingress of trinitarian prayer.
- A sense of gratitude for what they have received.
- A leaving of sin and self—with eyes on Christ: vision is other oriented.
- A desire for a new way—to live and to be.

- An ability to set aside being absorbed in their own vision because they want to be absorbed in God's viewpoint.
- A realization that Jesus has given God glory better than anyone else.
- A sense that they are loved as the sinner they are.
- A wanting to give all to be with Christ.
- Knowledge that their fate is tied up with the life of Christ.
- The experience of Christ's love for them even as sinners.
- A heart that will only be filled by Christ.
- A sign of hope that is emerging from within.
- A feeling they are ready for an infusion of the life of Christ—they want to be with Him.

Retreatants are ready for the Second Week when they

- Are telling you more and more about their colloquies—and how important they are to them.
- Don't think they have ever had a relationship with Jesus, and they want that.
- Say, "Jesus is the measure of what I have wanted all my life."
- Want to follow Jesus.
- Say, "Jesus, show me where I'm going—I'm confused."
- Are now feeling that Jesus loves them.
- Want their hearts to be filled only by Christ.
- Feel they can't do it all by themselves. They want to let Jesus lead them.
- Want to do something about this Christ on the cross (paragraph 53).
- See the depth of evil—its power—and how it spreads: one evil action creates more and more evil and destruction of lives.
- Experience the gift of anger arising within and so see Christ as angry at evil.

- Ask, "How will Christ conquer it? A curiosity...a need to see this...a need to know it: How are you going to handle it, Lord, to deal with it in me?"
- Are released from the struggle with evil—experience joy—a freedom from evil.
- Wonder and are amazed: "Why did you did this for me? What is this all about, Lord, that You did this for me?"
- Say, "I want to do this...to go with You—I don't have to, but I want to."
- Do not dread: "You will TAKE something from me if I give myself to You."
- Are tired and bored with the way that they look at things.
- Want to be healed by Christ and know that only He alone can do it.
- Want to enter the Scriptures not as an "outsider" but in Scripture's living reality in them...in their life.

Chapter 7

THE KINGDOM MEDITATION

From the text of the Spiritual Exercises of St. Ignatius of Loyola:

THE KINGDOM OF CHRIST

91. THE CALL OF AN EARTHLY KING

This will help us to contemplate the life of the eternal king

PRAYER. The preparatory prayer will be as usual.

FIRST PRELUDE. This is a mental representation of the place. Here it will be to see in imagination the synagogues, villages, and towns where Christ our Lord preached.

SECOND PRELUDE. I will ask for the grace I desire. Here it will be to ask of our Lord the grace not to be deaf to His call, but prompt and diligent to accomplish His most holy will.

FIRST PART

92. FIRST POINT. This will be to place before my mind a human king, chosen by God our Lord Himself, to whom all Christian princes and people pay homage and obedience.

93. SECOND POINT. This will be to consider the address this king makes to all his subjects, with the words: "It is my will to conquer all the lands of the infidel. Therefore, whoever wishes to join with me in this enterprise must be content with the same food, drink, clothing, etc., as mine. So, too, he must work with me by day, and watch with me by night, etc., that as he has had a share in the toil with me, afterwards, he may share in the victory with me."

94. THIRD POINT. Consider what the answer of good subjects ought to be to a king so generous and noble-minded, and consequently, if anyone would refuse the invitation of such a king, how justly he would deserve to be condemned by the whole world, and looked upon as an ignoble knight.

SECOND PART

The second part of this exercise will consist in applying the example of the earthly king mentioned above to Christ our Lord according to the following points:

95. FIRST POINT. If such a summons of an earthly king to his subjects deserves our attention, how much more worthy of consideration is Christ our Lord, the Eternal King, before whom is assembled the whole world. To all His summons goes forth, and to each one in particular He addresses the words: "It is my will to conquer the whole world and all my enemies, and thus to enter into the glory of my Father. Therefore, whoever wishes to join me in this enterprise must be willing to labor with me, that by following me in suffering, he may follow me in glory."

96. SECOND POINT. Consider that all persons who have judgment and reason will offer themselves entirely for this work.

97. THIRD POINT. Those who wish to give greater proof of their love, and to distinguish themselves in whatever concerns the

service of the eternal King and the Lord of all, will not only offer themselves entirely for the work, but will act against their sensuality and carnal and worldly love, and make offerings of greater value and of more importance in words such as these:

98. ETERNAL LORD OF ALL THINGS

Eternal Lord of all things, in the presence of Thy infinite goodness, and of Thy glorious mother, and of all the saints of Thy heavenly court, this is the offering of myself which I make with Thy favor and help. I protest that it is my earnest desire and my deliberate choice, provided only it is for Thy greater service and praise, to imitate Thee ill bearing all wrongs and all abuse and all poverty, both actual and spiritual, should Thy most holy majesty deign to choose and admit me to such a state and way of life.

NOTES

99. Note I. This exercise should be gone through twice during the day, that is, in the morning on rising, and an hour before dinner, or before supper.

Note II. During the Second Week and thereafter, it will be very profitable to read some passages from the Following of Christ, or from the Gospels, and from the Lives of the Saints.

A DAY OF REPOSE

A Day of Repose is part of the retreat—the retreatants need to know that

- There will be no phoning home or doing business. This is not a break from the retreat!
- Eucharistic celebration needs to be quiet and meditational.
- The Day of Repose prayer occurs two times, with morning and evening themes.

- ◆ The intention of this day is to thank God for the graces received during the retreat.
- ◆ Another possibility could be going over a favorite Scripture passage.
- ◆ Or one could read the Kingdom Meditation (paragraph 91).

- Do not go forward in the Spiritual Exercises and do not have a formal hour of prayer.
- A Day of Repose is to be a light relaxing day, as the retreatant has been in intense prayer for some days now.

THE KINGDOM MEDITATION (PARAGRAPH 91)

What is this? What is the grace of this exercise?

The Kingdom Meditation is right out of St. Ignatius's conversion process at Loyola, in the time of the conquests of Columbus, Magellan, and Cortez, and during the reign of Ferdinand and Isabella, all representing the kingdoms of this world. Then Francis, Dominic, and Benedict modeled Christ and His kingdom for Ignatius.

That Christ modulated Ignatius's dedication and desire for glory from an earthly kingdom to Himself and His kingdom are the points of this Kingdom Meditation:

- Magnanimity of heart: how much more worthy is Christ's call?
- Greater proof of their love.
- You are not being "sent out alone," but are asked by Christ; called by Christ to be with Him—with the same "conditions" as he experiences. So this is real leadership…real fellowship.
- Where is "the kingdom"? What is my role?

- Real leadership is Jesus saying, "Come with Me," and the "conditions" are the same for the retreatants and for Jesus: His conditions are for me as well.
- A kind of loneliness is really a temptation, like I'm going to be alone in ministry—no, you are with Christ…it is Christ's ministry, Christ's call, Christ's kingdom, not the retreatant's—the retreatant is with Him always.

The Gospels were written for a certain local situation of a specific community, and the life of Jesus is being applied to a specific human situational problem. This is the Kingdom Meditation as well. In the same way, there is a specific call by Christ to be lived out in our time and space for a certain reason for God's People. It is the same inner call except it's now in the twenty-first century. This is a living call now…today—a PARTICULAR CALL, AND TO EACH ONE IN PARTICULAR.

The Kingdom Meditation deepens and stretches. Paragraph 53, the colloquy of the First Exercise of the First Week: "What have I done for Christ? What am I doing for Christ? What will I do for Christ?"

Questions:

- How does it work?
- And how does it function?

The Kingdom Meditation functions like the First Principle and Foundation. It is a gauge to see if you are ready and capable to move into the Second Week of the Spiritual Exercises. If it is true for a temporal king, how much more will I do this for Christ the King? The attention a political leader gets is a bit disgraceful. Where is the Kingdom Meditation attention directed? Jesus says, "Come with Me." The conditions are the same for me as for Jesus. This is real leadership.

What are the signs that the retreatants are asking you to give them the Kingdom Meditation?

- The signs are the same as the signs one is asking to go into the Second Week.
- Where is your heart NOW? Then paragraph 98...recast your own heart in your own words.

How do you give the Kingdom Meditation?

- If Mother Teresa or the pope called you up and asked you to do something, how would you feel?

  - Just to be asked is an honor.
  - Elated, proud, freed—you would do it because the pope asked you. You are honored to be asked. You are honored because you are called.

- Who is someone you admire—hero worship—someone who for you is a hero?
- Infatuation with a movie star: you come home from the movies and you "play" them with a fondness.
- What about the high price to be with Jesus?
- Do you have the friendship of a vassal and lord and king? To be a KNIGHT is a DEEPER RELATIONSHIP...a deeper love and dedication.
- Scriptures to consider:

  - Luke 5:1–11, 27–28; and 6:12–16, *call of the Twelve*
  - 1 Corinthians 4:9–13, *called and rejected*
  - Matthew 15:24–28, *conditions of following Christ*
  - John 4:1–42, *Samaritan woman*
  - Matthew 25:31–48, *the last judgment*
  - Luke 9:23–26, *conditions of discipleship*
  - John 10:1–21, *the Good Shepherd*
  - Matthew 5:1–12, *the Beatitudes*

- ◆ Matthew 13:12–16, *Who do you say that I am?*
- ◆ Colossians 1, *Christ is the Head of all creation*
- ◆ Philippians 3, *the way of Christ*

For the First Part, have the retreatants write out what they admire in a person.

- What are the qualifications of this person?
- Write out your own response.
- In the relationship of a knight to his medieval king there was deep personal loyalty.

  The king would take the hands of the knight in his hands in a deep gesture of commitment. This is used in the liturgy of ordination to priesthood where the bishop takes the hands of the priest in his own hands as the priest promises obedience to his bishop ordinary.
- Consider the possibility of the sacrament of reconciliation at this time.

  - ◆ Effective penances? Who would you like to prayer for? Please pray for someone else who is suffering.
  - ◆ Pray for a person you have offended.
  - ◆ Pray for a person who offended you: "pray for those who persecute you…for your enemies."

- Consider also—what about…

  - ◆ Midnight meditation?
  - ◆ General confession?
  - ◆ Effective Scripture?
  - ◆ Effective procedures?

Are you as a director experiencing any new elements of the grace of the First Week?

Chapter 8

THE GRACE AND STRUCTURE OF THE SECOND WEEK OF THE SPIRITUAL EXERCISES

From the text of the Spiritual Exercises of St. Ignatius of Loyola:

101. FIRST DAY AND FIRST CONTEMPLATION

This is a contemplation on the incarnation. After the preparatory prayer and three preludes there are three points and a colloquy

PRAYER. The usual preparatory prayer.

102. FIRST PRELUDE. This will consist in calling to mind the history of the subject I have to contemplate. Here it will be how the Three Divine Persons look down upon the whole expanse or circuit of all the earth, filled with human beings. Since They see that all are going down to hell, They decree in Their eternity that the Second Person should become man to save the human race. So when the fullness of time had come, They send the Angel Gabriel to our Lady. Cf. # 262.

103. SECOND PRELUDE. This is a mental representation of the place. It will be here to see the great extent of the surface of the earth, inhabited by so many different peoples, and especially to see the house and room of our Lady in the city of Nazareth in the province of Galilee.

104. THIRD PRELUDE. This is to ask for what I desire. Here it will be to ask for an intimate knowledge of our Lord, who has become man for me, that I may love Him more and follow Him more closely.

105. *Note*

Attention must be called to the following point. The same preparatory prayer without any change, as was mentioned in the beginning, and the three preludes, with such changes of form as the subject demands, are to be made during this Week and during the others that follow.

106. FIRST POINT. This will be to see the different persons:

First, those on the face of the earth, in such great diversity in dress and in manner of acting. Some are white, some black; some at peace, and some at war; some weeping, some laughing; some well, some sick; some coming into the world, and some dying; etc.

Secondly, I will see and consider the Three Divine Persons seated on the royal dais or throne of the Divine Majesty. They look down upon the whole surface of the earth, and behold all nations in great blindness, going down to death and descending into hell.

Thirdly, I will see our Lady and the angel saluting her.

I will reflect upon this to draw profit from what I see.

107. SECOND POINT. This will be to listen to what the persons on the face of the earth say, that is, how they speak to one

another, swear and blaspheme, etc. I will also hear what the Divine Persons say, that is, "Let us work the redemption of the human race," etc. Then I will listen to what the angel and our Lady say. Finally, I will reflect upon all I hear to draw profit from their words.

108. THIRD POINT. This will be to consider what the persons on the face of the earth do, for example, wound, kill, and go down to hell. Also, what the Divine Persons do, namely, work the most holy Incarnation, etc. Likewise, what the Angel and our Lady do; how the Angel carries out his office of ambassador; and how our Lady humbles herself and offers thanks to the Divine Majesty.

Then I shall reflect upon all to draw some fruit from each of these details.

109. COLLOQUY. The exercise should be closed with a colloquy. I will think over what I ought to say to the Three Divine Persons, or to the eternal Word incarnate, or to His Mother, our Lady. According to the light that I have received, I will beg for grace to follow and imitate more closely our Lord, who has just become man for me.

Close with an *Our Father.*

110. THE SECOND CONTEMPLATION

The Nativity

PRAYER. The usual preparatory prayer.

111. FIRST PRELUDE. This is the history of the mystery. Here it will be that our Lady, about nine months with child, and, as may be piously believed, seated on an ass, set out from Nazareth. She was accompanied by Joseph and a maid, who was leading an ox. They are going to Bethlehem to pay the tribute that Caesar imposed on those lands. Cf. # 264.

112. SECOND PRELUDE. This is a mental representation of the place. It will consist here in seeing in imagination the way from Nazareth to Bethlehem. Consider its length, its breadth; whether level, or through valleys and over hills. Observe also the place or cave where Christ is born; whether big or little; whether high or low; and how it is arranged.

113. THIRD PRELUDE. This is the same as in the preceding contemplation and identical in form with it.

114. FIRST POINT. This will consist in seeing the persons, namely, our Lady, St. Joseph, the maid, and the Child Jesus after His birth. I will make myself a poor little unworthy slave, and as though present, look upon them, contemplate them, and serve them in their needs with all possible homage and reverence.

Then I will reflect on myself that I may reap some fruit.

115. SECOND POINT. This will be to consider, observe, and contemplate what the persons are saying, and then to reflect on myself and draw some fruit from it.

116 THIRD POINT. This will be to see and consider what they are doing, for example, making the journey and laboring that our Lord might be born in extreme poverty, and that after many labors, after hunger, thirst, heat, and cold, after insults and outrages, He might die on the cross, and all this for me.

Then I will reflect and draw some spiritual fruit from what I have seen.

117. COLLOQUY. Close with a colloquy as in the preceding contemplation, and with the *Our Father*.

118. THE THIRD CONTEMPLATION

This will be a repetition of the first and second exercises

After the preparatory prayer and the three preludes, a repetition of the First and Second Exercises will be made. In doing this, attention should always be given to some more important parts in which one has experienced understanding, consolation, or desolation.

Close the exercise with a colloquy and an *Our Father*.

119. In this repetition and in all those which follow, the same order of proceeding should be observed as in the repetitions of the First Week. The subject matter is changed but the same form is observed.

120. THE FOURTH CONTEMPLATION

This will consist in a repetition of the first and second exercises in the same way as in the repetition given above

121. THE FIFTH CONTEMPLATION

This will consist in applying the five senses to the matter of the first and second contemplations

After the preparatory prayer and three preludes, it will be profitable with the aid of the imagination to apply the five senses to the subject matter of the First and Second Contemplation in the following manner:

122. FIRST POINT. This consists in seeing in imagination the persons, and in contemplating and meditating in detail the circumstances in which they are, and then in drawing some fruit from what has been seen.

123. Second Point. This is to hear what they are saying, or what they might say, and then by reflecting on oneself to draw some profit from what has been heard.

124. Third Point. This is to smell the infinite fragrance, and taste the infinite sweetness of the divinity. Likewise, to apply these senses to the soul and its virtues, and to all according to the person we are contemplating, and to draw fruit from this.

125. Fourth Point. This is to apply the sense of touch, for example, by embracing and kissing the place where the persons stand or are seated, always taking care to draw some fruit from this.

126. COLLOQUY. Conclude with a colloquy and with an *Our Father* as in the First and Second Contemplations.

NOTES

127. Note I. Attention must be called to the following point. Throughout this Week and the subsequent Weeks, I ought to read only the mystery that I am immediately to contemplate. Hence, I should not read any mystery that is not to be used on that day or at that hour, lest the consideration of one mystery interfere with the contemplation of the other.

128. Note II. The First Exercise on the Incarnation should take place at midnight, the second at daybreak, the third about the time of Mass, the fourth near the time of Vespers, and the fifth an hour before supper. The same order should be observed on all the following days.

129. Note III. If the exercitant is old or weak, or even when strong, if he has come from the First Week rather exhausted, it should be noted that in this Second Week it would be better, at

least at times, not to rise at midnight. Then one contemplation would be in the morning, another would be at the time of Mass, a third before dinner, with one repetition of them at the time of Vespers, and the Application of the Senses before supper.

130. NOTE IV. Of the ten Additional Directions given during the First Week, the following should be changed during the Second Week: the second, the sixth, the seventh, and part of the tenth.

The second will be that as soon as I awake, I should place before my mind the subject of the contemplation with the desire to know better the eternal Word Incarnate in order to serve and follow Him more closely.

The sixth will be to call to mind frequently the mysteries of the life of Christ our Lord from the Incarnation to the place or mystery I am contemplating.

The seventh will be that the exercitant take care to darken his room, or admit the light; to make use of pleasant or disagreeable weather, in as far as he perceives that it may be of profit, and help to find what he desires.

In the observance of the tenth Additional Direction, the exercitant must conduct himself as the mysteries he is contemplating demand. Some call for penance; others do not.

Thus, all ten Additional Directions are to be observed with great care.

131. NOTE V. In all the exercises, except the one at midnight and the one in the morning, an equivalent of the second Additional Direction should be observed as follows:

As soon as I recall that it is time for the exercise in which I ought to engage, before proceeding to it, I will call to mind, where I am going, before whom I am to appear, and briefly sum up the exercise. Then after observing the third Additional Direction, I shall enter upon the exercise.

132. SECOND DAY

On the second day, for the first and second contemplations, the Presentation in the Temple, # 268, and the Flight into Exile in Egypt, # 269, should be used. Two repetitions will be made of these contemplations, and the Application of the Senses, in the same way as was done on the preceding day.

133. *Note*

Sometimes it will be profitable, even when the exercitant is strong and well-disposed, to make some changes from the second day to the fourth inclusive in order to attain better what is desired. Thus, the first contemplation would be the one on rising. Then there would be a second about the time of Mass, a repetition about the time of Vespers, and the Application of the Senses before supper.

134. THIRD DAY

On the third day use the contemplations on the Obedience of the Child Jesus to His parents, # 271, and the Finding of the Child Jesus in the Temple, # 272. Then will follow the two repetitions and the Application of the Senses.

WHAT IS THE STRUCTURE AND THE MEANING OF THE SECOND WEEK OF THE SPIRITUAL EXERCISES?

Pre-Note

LET US BEGIN WITH AN EPISTEMOLOGICAL PRINCIPLE: What I am coming to know determines the methodology of how I come to know it.

If you want to know the multiplication tables, you memorize them:

$$2 \times 2 = 4$$

If you want to know a person, you simply be with that person in many varied settings and experiences, such as shopping, dining, working, painting, cleaning, playing sports, going on picnics, and traveling.

The method of coming to know Jesus is the prayer of contemplation.

- Contemplation is different than meditation.
- Contemplation is getting to know a person. Michelangelo lived with the stone in his studio before he carved his David.

What are the signs that a person is asking for the gift of the Second Week of the Spiritual Exercises?

- The parameters of formal prayer time are evanescing.

    - Retreatants can spend a long time on a small detail.
    - What the Holy Spirit is working in them is the gift of prayer of the Second Week: the dispositions for the gift of Ignatian contemplation.

- I want to enter *into* Scripture; I do not want to know it as an outsider.

HOW DOES ST. IGNATIUS GIVE THE SECOND WEEK OF THE SPIRITUAL EXERCISES?

- Paragraph 128: Gives the order of the five exercises in a normal day.

- Paragraph 119: "Subject matter is changed but the same form is used."
- Paragraphs 101–31: What is the interior meaning of the method St. Ignatius uses?
- Paragraph 119: The repetitions of the Second Week are to be done like the ones in the First Week (paragraphs 62, 63, 64).

  ◆ **Third Exercise**: A deeper knowledge (as paragraph 63), a feeling of the disorder of my actions—here in the Second Week—a deeper feeling knowledge of Jesus as a person.

  ◆ **Fourth Exercise**: Paragraph 64 brings in the use of the memory, so you see over and over the same thing as a HABIT…you see a PATTERN.

    ▪ Here in the Second Week, we are looking for CONSISTENCY. It takes on a new meaning to a call—the membranes of a call of Christ: it is an embryo… embryonic at this time.

    ▪ We have the vague sinews here of a life—a movement—we have to repeat the consolations and desolations to have it become clear…to take shape… to have it take on flesh and bones…to have the bones grow so I can see the form. Therefore, repetitions are necessary.

- A deeper knowledge—so the same structure as the First Week—the life of Christ brings up my life in the present.
- Same principle as paragraph 53—I can't look at my life alone—I need to look at my life through the eyes of the life of Christ: this is the gift of Ignatian contemplation.

  ◆ Here Christ chooses how I am to look at my own life.
  ◆ You as a director can see what needs to be looked at, but let God bring up what God's wants to bring up… through the contemplation on the life of Christ.

◆ The path a person is to take and traverse must come from Christ, not the individuals themselves…and not from you, the director.

WHAT IS THE GRACE OF THE SECOND WEEK OF THE SPIRITUAL EXERCISES?

When the retreatant's life comes up while looking at and contemplating Christ's life:

● The director's job is always to check and investigate and monitor that the retreatants' thoughts and ideas about their life are not coming from themselves or the director but from Christ in their contemplation.

● The retreatants' life must be in God's hands, not in their own, as retreatants would tear themselves apart with guilt or some such feeling…same principle as the First Week, paragraph 53.

● This DEACTIVATES you as the director of the retreat and instates Christ as the Director of the retreat because God chooses what the retreatants will work on…not you, the director.

◆ The gift of counseling, which all directors have, allows a director to see the problems that retreatants have, as well as to prioritize them in the order of severity, and instantly tabulate how many hours of therapy it would take them to resolve them. All of this is absolutely true, but it becomes deactivated in the face of Jesus determining what retreatants will work on through the consolations and desolations of their contemplations on his earthly life.

◆ This situates the director's job: to make sure the work of the retreatants' life and direction comes from Christ and not from the director…and not from the retreatants' agenda.

◆ Not only does the director have to become deactivated as choosing what to decide to work on and how, but the retreatants themselves have to become deactivated as directors of their own retreats. So as to let Christ choose the decision to be made and what to reform or not to reform.

● Let Christ live his life in you.

Application of the Senses: Paragraph 121

● What is it? Ignatius employs the imagination here.
● The senses are a way into Christ more personally…a one-ness with mystery…a way into the mystery of Christ.
● It is like sitting on the back porch at twilight with Jesus in a rocking chair with a cup of coffee reminiscing about the day and about what happened in prayer…remembering.
● Imagine driving back from a wonderful day at a mountain lake with a friend—in silence—and every now and then one says to the other, "Wasn't the lake beautiful today?" and you respond, "Yes, it was, and the trees were so beautiful." The other says yes, then you both lapse into silence remembering…going over your memories together and remembering them as you go home.

Week Two Notes

IMAGINATION: Imagination is the highest form of intelligence. A Harvard study examined the works from Adam to the present day to see who was the most intelligent person who ever lived. They used two axes of investigation: (1) simplicity of work and (2) complexity of work. The result was Mozart. The function of the "imagination" is to unite the head with hand and heart.

See the sensuality, for example, in the Fourth Point: "embracing and kissing." This is a "logic of the heart" prayer. A sense of meaning means a "familiarity" with the person of Jesus. THIS IS A SENSE OF MEANING. It is time for the Triple Colloquy, paragraph 109.

Signs a person is asking for the Second Week gift

- The parameters of formal prayer time begin to evanesce.

  ◆ The retreatant can spend a long time on a small detail.
  ◆ What the Holy Spirit is working in them is the gift of prayer of the Second Week: the dispositions for the gift of Ignatian contemplation.

- The retreatant wants to enter *into* Scripture: I don't want to know it as an outsider.
- The retreatant wants to be with Jesus, walk with Jesus.

These dispositions mean the retreatant is ready for the Second Week material. A retreatant is saying, "Give me this material":

- Generosity becomes a perduring affect—from paragraph 53 colloquy: This perduring affect may extend into the past of the retreatant five years, ten years, twenty-five years, or fifty years back into their life. This may be emerging from repression away from one's consciousness in order to be seen, and the retreatants may now enter this generosity freely.
- Depression and disappointment: sorrow and contrition continuing on from the First Week—this is also a perduring affect...something is there...in the retreatants, to be done—to be surfaced. This Second Week material will surface it—bring these contours to light.

Some change suggests itself from contemplating the life of Christ. The retreatant starts talking of humility as attractive. They are seeing the world and wanting to do something: "What should I do?"

They go on to say things like

- I'm searching for a way to lead my life.
- How am I personally tempted? It's not going to be to kill the mailman…so how about me?
- Satan offers nothing but false promises…God offers lasting joy and real peace. (On hearing this, start them on the Two Standards because they are in it already.) And they shed tears thinking of the humble Jesus.
- I need real humility…not fake and false humility.
- I need to reconstruct my life.
- I'm dissatisfied where I am.
- I want to simplify my life.
- I want to control everything in my life, and I'm tired of doing that.
- There is much too much self in my life.
- I'm bored with taking control of the retreat.
- I'm just not happy.
- My controlling my own life hasn't worked.
- How have I been deceived?
- Self-serving? I've been using my gifts to serve myself.
- (If married…) I'm too busy, and I'm trashing my marriage and I'm not having the children I want to have.
- I'm always taking control of everything, and I end up empty and exhausted.

There is "something to be done" emerging: a gerundive structure—an "embryo"—something that is embryonic emerging…we don't know if it's a boy or a girl yet…whether to paint the room pink or blue…a reformation of life issue, which is still not clear (as the Spiritual Exercises are really only to make clear and clarify what

Christ is already doing to a person—not to engender dispositions as much as to identify clearly what Christ is already doing).

Clarity brings power over dynamics and dispositions and movements that we are buffeted by and do not understand their meanings and origins…as we are here to glorify Christ and serve our Creator and Lord, and the Lord's movement within the retreatants.

WHAT IS THE GIFT AND THE GRACE OF THE APPLICATION OF THE SENSES PRAYER?

- This prayer takes hold as it ends in a sense of meaning.
- This prayer ends in an intuition: it "makes sense"…in a sense of meaning.
- This knowledge is a felt knowledge—felt and rooted in sense data as the way one would get up as a kid in the morning and sense that the day is sunny from feeling the sound of the day…the hum of the city.
- In this prayer from all the sense experience, there is a "meaning."
- This is SENTIR…I feel it "in my bones"…my body knows it.
- Do you know what it's like to live in a home? If you say yes, that yes is a felt knowledge from many sense images, experiences, and memories. This is felt thought.
- From the phantasms and images and experiences from my day, an intuitive knowledge comes: this is the meaning of the Spanish word SENTIR.
- This is a "logic of the heart" knowledge.
- "Now I know what it means"—an "aha" experience.
- NOW I KNOW WHAT IT MEANS…here imagination unites one's head and one's heart.

Art is 98 percent work—the next block of material will only reveal its riches with a meticulous procedure of work. For paragraphs 135–89, you must get clear about what St. Ignatius is saying.

Paragraph 135: Introduction to the different states of life

From the text of the Spiritual Exercises of St. Ignatius of Loyola:

135. INTRODUCTION TO THE CONSIDERATION OF DIFFERENT STATES OF LIFE

The example which Christ our Lord gave of the first state of life, which is that of observing the Commandments, has already been considered in meditating on His obedience to His parents. The example of the second state, which is that of evangelical perfection, has also been considered, when He remained in the temple and left His foster father and His Mother to devote Himself exclusively to the service of His eternal Father.

While continuing to contemplate His life, let us begin to investigate and ask in what kind of life or in what state His Divine Majesty wishes to make use of us.

Therefore, as some introduction to this, in the next exercise, let us consider the intention of Christ our Lord, and on the other hand, that of the enemy of our human nature. Let us also see how we ought to prepare ourselves to arrive at perfection in whatever state or way of life God our Lord may grant us to choose.

136. THE FOURTH DAY

A MEDITATION ON TWO STANDARDS

The one of Christ, our supreme leader and lord, the other of Lucifer, the deadly enemy of our human nature

PRAYER. The usual preparatory prayer.

137. FIRST PRELUDE. This is the history. Here it will be that Christ calls and wants all beneath His standard, and Lucifer, on the other hand, wants all under his.

138. SECOND PRELUDE. This is a mental representation of the place. It will be here to see a great plain, comprising the whole region about Jerusalem, where the sovereign Commander-in-Chief of all the good is Christ our Lord; and another plain about the region of Babylon, where the chief of the enemy is Lucifer.

139. THIRD PRELUDE. This is to ask for what I desire. Here it will be to ask for a knowledge of the deceits of the rebel chief and help to guard myself against them; and also to ask for a knowledge of the true life exemplified in the sovereign and true Commander, and the grace to imitate Him.

FIRST PART

THE STANDARD OF SATAN

140. FIRST POINT. Imagine you see the chief of all the enemy in the vast plain about Babylon, seated on a great throne of fire and smoke, his appearance inspiring horror and terror.

141. SECOND POINT. Consider how he summons innumerable demons, and scatters them, some to one city and some to another, throughout the whole world, so that no province, no place, no state of life, no individual is overlooked.

142. THIRD POINT. Consider the address he makes to them, how he goads them on to lay snares for men and bind them with chains. First, they are to tempt them to covet riches (as Satan himself is accustomed to do in most cases) that they may the more easily attain the empty honors of this world, and then come to overweening pride.

The first step, then, will be riches; the second, honor; the third, pride. From these three steps the evil one leads to all other vices.

SECOND PART

THE STANDARD OF CHRIST

143. In a similar way, we are to picture to ourselves the sovereign and true Commander, Christ our Lord.

144. FIRST POINT. Consider Christ our Lord, standing in a lowly place in a great plain about the region of Jerusalem, His appearance beautiful and attractive.

145. SECOND POINT. Consider how the Lord of all the world chooses so many persons, apostles, disciples, etc., and sends them throughout the whole world to spread His sacred doctrine among all men, no matter what their state or condition.

146. THIRD POINT. Consider the address which Christ our Lord makes to all His servants and friends whom He sends on this enterprise, recommending to them to seek to help all, first by attracting them to the highest spiritual poverty, and should it please the Divine Majesty, and should He deign to choose them for it, even to actual poverty. Secondly, they should lead them to a desire for insults and contempt, for from these springs humility.

Hence, there will be three steps: the first, poverty as opposed to riches; the second, insults or contempt as opposed to the honor of this world; the third, humility as opposed to pride. From these three steps, let them lead men to all other virtues.

147. COLLOQUY. A colloquy should be addressed to our Lady, asking her to obtain for me from her Son and Lord the grace to be received under His standard, first in the highest spiritual poverty, and should the Divine Majesty be pleased thereby, and deign to choose and accept me, even in actual poverty; secondly, in bearing insults and wrongs, thereby to imitate Him

better, provided only I can suffer these without sin on the part of another, and without offense of the Divine Majesty. Then I will say the Hail Mary.

SECOND COLLOQUY. This will be to ask her Son to obtain the same favors for me from the Father. Then I will say, Soul of Christ.

THIRD COLLOQUY. This will be to beg the Father to grant me the same graces. Then I will say the *Our Father*.

148. *Note*

This exercise will be made at midnight and again in the morning. There will be two repetitions of the same exercise, one about the time of Mass and the other about the time of Vespers. The same three colloquies, with our Lady, with her Son, and with the Father, will close all these exercises as well as the one on the Three Classes of Men, which follows an hour before supper.

Paragraph 135: Introduction to the different states of life

- What will set this off? The grace of Ignatian contemplation …from some episode in the life of Christ. Christ chooses the episode and what to make a choice about: THIS IS WHAT I HAVE BEEN CHOSEN FOR…CHOSEN BY CHRIST….
- What does "the enemy of our human nature" mean?

The Two Standards: As an introduction to considering different states of life:

- How sin works—how grace works.

- This is a tool to make us more sensitive so I can listen to what Christ is moving me to.
- Look at the VERBS in this meditation.
- The Two Standards is not about a choice between Jesus and Satan, but it is about the means and strategies of Jesus and the means and strategies of Satan. It is about knowledge... the gift of knowledge of the strategies of Satan and the knowledge of the strategies of Jesus: the "ways" of each.

Knowledge of the deceits of Satan:

- Riches: What kind of riches?
- Binding a person by coveting riches.
- If you go for riches, honors, and pride, you get to the top and it's pretty empty because that's all you get—riches, honors, pride.

Knowledge of the true-life example of Christ:

- Jesus: freedom for ministry.
- Satan: riches, honor, pride.
- The issue is not riches, honors, pride. It is where this is going...the connection and movement between them—the direction and current of the movement to being possessed by these and not being free to serve the will and kingdom of Christ.
- Riches are not necessarily bad, for they can be used to serve people. Honors are not necessarily bad, as for example, Mother Teresa received the Nobel Peace Prize. Pride can be not necessarily bad, as you can take pride in your work.
- An updated meaning of pride: I'm the center of all, the source of all. As in, "I'm in charge of the retreat." "I'm in charge of everything in my life."
    - ◆ Christ's example is of poverty, insults, and humiliation.

- An updated meaning of humility: God is the center of all, and I receive everything from God.
  - ◆ For example: the sun revolves around the earth versus heliocentricity, where the earth revolves around the sun—a totally different and new worldview.

Colloquy of the Two Standards

This is the most dominant and important hinge point colloquy in the Spiritual Exercises as it is returned to and is to be used in every colloquy of the Second and Third Weeks. For example, it is used in paragraph 189, the surrender of self-will; also in paragraph 149 about Three Classes of Persons; and paragraphs 165–68 about Three Kinds of Humility.

Paragraph 156 says to use the Triple Colloquy of the Meditation on the Two Standards. Paragraph 159 says the fifth day and all days of the Second Week will conclude with the Triple Colloquy.

Paragraph 136—on the fourth day—the Two Standards is done four times with the Three Classes of Persons as the Fifth Exercise, as a Repetition.

Paragraph 148 notes,

- The first at midnight
- The second in the morning
- The third is a repetition
- The fourth is a repetition
- The fifth is the Three Classes of Persons, paragraph 149: The Triple Colloquy

From the text of the Spiritual Exercises of St. Ignatius of Loyola:

149. THREE CLASSES OF MEN

This is a meditation for the same fourth day to choose that which is better

PRAYER. The usual preparatory prayer.

150. FIRST PRELUDE. This is the history of the Three Classes of Men. Each of them has acquired ten thousand ducats, but not entirely as they should have, for the love of God. They all wish to save their souls and find peace in God our Lord by ridding themselves of the burden arising from the attachment to the sum acquired, which impedes the attainment of this end.

151. SECOND PRELUDE. This is a mental representation of the place. Here it will be to behold myself standing in the presence of God our Lord and of all His saints, that I may know and desire what is more pleasing to His Divine Goodness.

152. THIRD PRELUDE. This is to ask for what I desire. Here it will be to beg for the grace to choose what is more for the glory of His Divine Majesty and the salvation of my soul.

153. THE FIRST CLASS. They would like to rid themselves of the attachment they have to the sum acquired in order to find peace in God our Lord and assure their salvation, but the hour of death comes, and they have not made use of any means.

154. THE SECOND CLASS. They want to rid themselves of the attachment, but they wish to do so in such a way that they retain what they have acquired, so that God is to come to what they desire, and they do not decide to give up the sum of money in order to go to God, though this would be the better way for them.

155. THE THIRD CLASS. These want to rid themselves of the attachment, but they wish to do so in such a way that they desire neither to retain nor to relinquish the sum acquired. They seek only to will and not will as God our Lord inspires

them, and as seems better for the service and praise of the Divine Majesty. Meanwhile, they will strive to conduct themselves as if every attachment to it had been broken. They will make efforts neither to want that, nor anything else, unless the service of God our Lord alone moves them to do so. As a result, the desire to be better able to serve God our Lord will be the cause of their accepting anything or relinquishing it.

156. THREEFOLD COLLOQUY. I will make use of the same three colloquies employed in the preceding contemplation on Two Standards.

Meditation: The Three Classes of Persons

- The Three Classes of Persons is like the First Exercise of the First Week in that it starts with "sin…out there…objective… out there in the world…away from me." Then it moves inward to "my personal sinfulness." Likewise, the Three Classes is a situation "out there" away from me, and then in the Second Week the movement is into within me and my reform or choice, personal to me, moving inward to me.
- To become free of the burden—the burden of my personal attachment (paragraph 150).
- The Three Classes of Persons is an inner test of the quality of freedom the retreatant has.
- They want not to be controlled by what they have…so that money is not the primary concern of their lives.
- This is a purification because all that I have, I have with impure motivations.
- First Class: PROCRASTINATORS…approach… WISHERS.
- Second Class: COMPROMISERS…approach… TALKERS.

- Third Class: DOERS…in freedom, approach…an exercise to set in shape in order to have Christ pick something for me to do…for Christ to live his life in me…**to will as Christ inspires me to will and to do.**
- Paragraph 155: FREEDOM…the Third Class.
- Paragraph 169.

The Fifth Day: Contemplation of Jesus leaving Nazareth, paragraph 158

This is done five times:

- Paragraph 164 is the same day: the Three Degrees of Humility is a consideration. Think it over, reviewing paragraphs 165, 166, and 167. This is really the Three Degrees of Love; that is, the three kinds of love, as the humility spoken of here is a consequence of love of Christ.

  - It follows from love of the person of Christ…wanting to be with Him…wanting to be identified with Him… wanting to imitate Him.
  - It is a deepening of the Three Classes of Persons, so giving this is really meant to be done in the third and fourth repetition of the fifth day.
  - It is going to the Jordan…leaving home…because the third and fourth repetitions are for "deepening" the graces, the consolations, and desolations.

- Paragraph 163: the choice of a way of life requires gaining information for a decision.
- Paragraph 189: involves reformation and surrender of will and intellect.
- Fold all into the Examination of Conscience—why? To let the grace live and breathe moment by moment.

The Three Classes of Persons—a repetition of the Two Standards

This is all happening on the fifth day because Jesus is leaving Nazareth and going to have an experience at the Jordan River.

This is

- Jesus's touchstone experience.
- Jesus's experience of mission.
- Jesus's experience of vocation.
- Jesus's choice…a mobile lifestyle.
- A state of life.
- An affirmation: "You are My Son" (Luke 3:21–22).
- Jesus's public life.

With the Three Degrees of Humility, the Three Degrees of Desire and Love come together:

- There is a law orientation…no mortal sin.
- Service wants more closeness, indifference…no venial sin.
- Will and likeness…a climate of desire.

Thomas Green, SJ, wrote about hating to go to the hospital, but his mother was there, dying, and therefore he loved the hospital after she died because she was there. It is the same with Christ—Christ had it, therefore, I want it…I love humiliations because Christ had them.

In another example, a nun who had cancer went into remission, and she said, "I miss it (cancer) because I was in union with Christ's suffering, and the bond I had with Him was so deep."

Choice of a way of life, paragraph 189:

How do you give this?

Keep in mind that the Spiritual Exercises can be given

- For a choice of a way of life…a major life decision.
- For a reformation of life…to open to Christ's deeper call.
- As a "school of the heart" retreat…to open to a deeper and closer relationship with Christ, our Creator and God.

Will the way the Spiritual Exercises are given affect the following material? I believe so.

How does St. Ignatius give this?

- Look at the strategies so that I can recognize them.
- Two Standards to address the intellect: knowledge.
- Three Classes of Persons to address the will: need for freedom.

How do you know when you have the gift of the Application of the Senses prayer?

- When your imagination of seeing, hearing, tasting, and touching end up in a sense of meaning, which is SENTIR.
- Paragraphs 261–312 bring a familiarity—a deeper knowledge and a deeper love.

Week Two Notes

IMAGINATION: Imagination is the highest form of intelligence. A Harvard study examined the works from Adam to the present day to see who was the most intelligent person who ever lived. They used two axes of investigation: (1) simplicity of work and (2) complexity of work. The result was Mozart. The function of the "imagination" is to unite the head with hand and heart. See the sensuality, for example, in the Fourth Point: "embracing and kissing." This is a "logic of the heart" prayer. A sense of meaning means a "familiarity" with the Person of Jesus. THIS IS A SENSE OF MEANING.

Chapter 9

THE TWO STANDARDS AND THE PATH THROUGH THE SECOND WEEK OF THE SPIRITUAL EXERCISES

From the text of the Spiritual Exercises of St. Ignatius of Loyola:

135. INTRODUCTION TO THE CONSIDERATION OF DIFFERENT STATES OF LIFE

The example which Christ our Lord gave of the first state of life, which is that of observing the Commandments, has already been considered in meditating on His obedience to His parents. The example of the second state, which is that of evangelical perfection, has also been considered, when He remained in the temple and left His foster father and His Mother to devote Himself exclusively to the service of His eternal Father.

While continuing to contemplate His life, let us begin to investigate and ask in what kind of life or in what state His Divine Majesty wishes to make use of us.

Therefore, as some introduction to this, in the next exercise, let us consider the intention of Christ our Lord, and on the other hand, that of the enemy of our human nature. Let us also see how we ought to prepare ourselves to arrive at perfection in whatever state or way of life God our Lord may grant us to choose.

136. THE FOURTH DAY

A MEDITATION ON TWO STANDARDS

The one of Christ, our supreme leader and lord, the other of Lucifer, the deadly enemy of our human nature

PRAYER. The usual preparatory prayer.

137. FIRST PRELUDE. This is the history. Here it will be that Christ calls and wants all beneath His standard, and Lucifer, on the other hand, wants all under his.

138. SECOND PRELUDE. This is a mental representation of the place. It will be here to see a great plain, comprising the whole region about Jerusalem, where the sovereign Commander-in-Chief of all the good is Christ our Lord; and another plain about the region of Babylon, where the chief of the enemy is Lucifer.

139. THIRD PRELUDE. This is to ask for what I desire. Here it will be to ask for a knowledge of the deceits of the rebel chief and help to guard myself against them; and also to ask for a knowledge of the true life exemplified in the sovereign and true Commander, and the grace to imitate Him.

FIRST PART

THE STANDARD OF SATAN

140. FIRST POINT. Imagine you see the chief of all the enemy in the vast plain about Babylon, seated on a great throne of fire and smoke, his appearance inspiring horror and terror.

141. SECOND POINT. Consider how he summons innumerable demons, and scatters them, some to one city and some to another, throughout the whole world, so that no province, no place, no state of life, no individual is overlooked.

142. THIRD POINT. Consider the address he makes to them, how he goads them on to lay snares for men and bind them with chains. First, they are to tempt them to covet riches (as Satan himself is accustomed to do in most cases) that they may the more easily attain the empty honors of this world, and then come to overweening pride.

The first step, then, will be riches, the second honor, the third pride. From these three steps the evil one leads to all other vices.

SECOND PART

THE STANDARD OF CHRIST

143. In a similar way, we are to picture to ourselves the sovereign and true Commander, Christ our Lord.

144. FIRST POINT. Consider Christ our Lord, standing in a lowly place in a great plain about the region of Jerusalem, His appearance beautiful and attractive.

145. SECOND POINT. Consider how the Lord of all the world chooses so many persons, apostles, disciples, etc., and sends them throughout the whole world to spread His sacred doctrine among all men, no matter what their state or condition.

146. THIRD POINT. Consider the address which Christ our Lord makes to all His servants and friends whom He sends on this enterprise, recommending to them to seek to help all, first by attracting them to the highest spiritual poverty, and should

it please the Divine Majesty, and should He deign to choose them for it, even to actual poverty. Secondly, they should lead them to a desire for insults and contempt, for from these springs humility.

Hence, there will be three steps: the first, poverty as opposed to riches; the second, insults or contempt as opposed to the honor of this world; the third, humility as opposed to pride. From these three steps, let them lead men to all other virtues.

147. COLLOQUY. A colloquy should be addressed to our Lady, asking her to obtain for me from her Son and Lord the grace to be received under His standard, first in the highest spiritual poverty, and should the Divine Majesty be pleased thereby, and deign to choose and accept me, even in actual poverty; secondly, in bearing insults and wrongs, thereby to imitate Him better, provided only I can suffer these without sin on the part of another, and without offense of the Divine Majesty. Then I will say the Hail Mary.

SECOND COLLOQUY. This will be to ask her Son to obtain the same favors for me from the Father. Then I will say, Soul of Christ.

THIRD COLLOQUY. This will be to beg the Father to grant me the same graces. Then I will say the *Our Father*.

148. *Note*

This exercise will be made at midnight and again in the morning. There will be two repetitions of the same exercise, one about the time of Mass and the other about the time of Vespers. The same three colloquies, with our Lady, with her Son, and with the Father, will close all these exercises as well as the one on the Three Classes of Men, which follows an hour before supper.

SECOND WEEK

149. THREE CLASSES OF PERSONS

This is a meditation for the same fourth day to choose that which is better

PRAYER. The usual preparatory prayer.

150. FIRST PRELUDE. This is the history of the Three Classes of Men. Each of them has acquired ten thousand ducats, but not entirely as they should have, for the love of God. They all wish to save their souls and find peace in God our Lord by ridding themselves of the burden arising from the attachment to the sum acquired, which impedes the attainment of this end.

151. SECOND PRELUDE. This is a mental representation of the place. Here it will be to behold myself standing in the presence of God our Lord and of all His saints, that I may know and desire what is more pleasing to His Divine Goodness.

152. THIRD PRELUDE. This is to ask for what I desire. Here it will be to beg for the grace to choose what is more for the glory of His Divine Majesty and the salvation of my soul.

153. THE FIRST CLASS. They would like to rid themselves of the attachment they have to the sum acquired in order to find peace in God our Lord and assure their salvation, but the hour of death comes, and they have not made use of any means.

154. THE SECOND CLASS. They want to rid themselves of the attachment, but they wish to do so in such a way that they retain what they have acquired, so that God is to come to what they desire, and they do not decide to give up the sum of money in order to go to God, though this would be the better way for them.

155. THE THIRD CLASS. These want to rid themselves of the attachment, but they wish to do so in such a way that they desire neither to retain nor to relinquish the sum acquired. They seek only to will and not will as God our Lord inspires them, and as seems better for the service and praise of the Divine Majesty. Meanwhile, they will strive to conduct themselves as if every attachment to it had been broken. They will make efforts neither to want that, nor anything else, unless the service of God our Lord alone moves them to do so. As a result, the desire to be better able to serve God our Lord will be the cause of their accepting anything or relinquishing it.

156. THREEFOLD COLLOQUY. I will make use of the same three colloquies employed in the preceding contemplation on Two Standards.

157. *Note*

It should be noted that when we feel an attachment opposed to actual poverty or a repugnance to it, when we are not indifferent to poverty and riches, it will be very helpful in order to overcome the inordinate attachment, even though corrupt nature rebel against it, to beg our Lord in the colloquies to choose us to serve Him in actual poverty. We should insist that we desire it, beg for it, plead for it, provided, of course, that it be for the service and praise of the Divine Goodness.

158. FIFTH DAY

The contemplation on the journey of Christ our Lord from Nazareth to the river Jordan and His baptism. Cf. # 273.

NOTES

159. NOTE I. This matter should be contemplated once at midnight, and again in the morning. There will be two repetitions

of it, one about the time of Mass and the other about the time of Vespers. Before supper there will be the Application of the Senses to the same mystery.

In each of these five exercises, there will be at the beginning, the preparatory prayer and the three preludes as was fully explained in the contemplations on the Incarnation and the Nativity. They will conclude with the three colloquies of the meditation on Three Classes of Men, or according to the note which follows this meditation.

160. NOTE II. The Particular Examination of Conscience after dinner and after supper will be made upon the faults and negligences with regard to the exercises of the day and on the Additional Directions. The same will be observed on the subsequent days.

161. SIXTH DAY

The contemplation will be on Christ our Lord's departure from the river Jordan for the desert and on the temptations. The same directions that were given for the fifth day will be followed here.

SEVENTH DAY

St. Andrew and others follow Christ our Lord. Cf. # 275.

EIGHTH DAY

The Sermon on the Mount, which is on the eight beatitudes. Cf. # 278.

NINTH DAY

Christ our Lord appears to His disciples on the waves of the sea. Cf. # 280.

TENTH DAY

Our Lord preaches in the temple. Cf. # 288.

ELEVENTH DAY

The raising of Lazarus. Cf. # 285.

TWELFTH DAY

Palm Sunday. Cf. # 287.

NOTES

162. NOTE I. Everyone, according to the time he wishes to devote to the contemplations of this Second Week, and according to his progress, may lengthen or shorten this Week.

If he wishes to lengthen it, let him take the mysteries of the Visitation of our Lady to Elizabeth, the Shepherds, the Circumcision of the Child Jesus, the Three Kings, and also others.

If he wishes to shorten the Week, he may omit even some of the mysteries that have been assigned. For they serve here to afford an introduction and method for better and more complete meditation later.

163. NOTE II. The treatment of the matter dealing with the Choice of a Way of Life will begin with the contemplation of our Lord's departure from Nazareth for the Jordan, taken inclusively, that is, on the Fifth Day, as is explained later.

164. NOTE III. Before entering upon the Choice of a Way of Life, in order that we may be filled with love of the true doctrine of Christ our Lord, it will be very useful to consider attentively the following Three Kinds of Humility. These should be thought over from time to time during the whole day, and the three colloquies should also be added as will be indicated further on.

SECOND WEEK

THREE KINDS OF HUMILITY

165. THE FIRST KIND OF HUMILITY. This is necessary for salvation. It consists in this, that as far as possible I so subject and humble myself as to obey the law of God our Lord in all things, so that not even were I made lord of all creation, or to save my life here on earth, would I consent to violate a commandment, whether divine or human, that binds me under pain of mortal sin.

166. THE SECOND KIND OF HUMILITY. This is more perfect than the first. I possess it if my attitude of mind is such that I neither desire nor am I inclined to have riches rather than poverty, to seek honor rather than dishonor, to desire a long life rather than a short life, provided only in either alternative I would promote equally the service of God our Lord and the salvation of my soul. Besides this indifference, this second kind of humility supposes that not for all creation, nor to save my life, would I consent to commit a venial sin.

167. THE THIRD KIND OF HUMILITY. This is the most perfect kind of humility. It consists in this. If we suppose the first and second kind attained, then whenever the praise and glory of the Divine Majesty would be equally served, in order to imitate and be in reality more like Christ our Lord, I desire and choose poverty with Christ poor, rather than riches; insults with Christ loaded with them, rather than honors; I desire to be accounted as worthless and a fool for Christ, rather than to be esteemed as wise and prudent in this world. So Christ was treated before me.

168. *Note*

If one desires to attain this third kind of humility, it will help very much to use the three colloquies at the close of the meditation on the three Classes of Men mentioned above. He should beg our Lord to deign to choose him for this third kind of humility, which is higher and better, that he may the more imitate and serve Him, provided equal or greater praise and service be given to the Divine Majesty.

169. INTRODUCTION TO MAKING A CHOICE OF A WAY OF LIFE

In every good choice, as far as depends on us, our intention must be simple. I must consider only the end for which I am created, that is, for the praise of God our Lord and for the salvation of my soul. Hence, whatever I choose must help me to this end for which I am created.

I must not subject and fit the end to the means, but the means to the end. Many first choose marriage, which is a means, and secondarily the service of God our Lord in marriage, though the service of God is the end. So also others first choose to have benefices, and afterwards to serve God in them. Such persons do not go directly to God, but want God to conform wholly to their inordinate attachments. Consequently, they make of the end a means, and of the means an end. As a result, what they ought to seek first, they seek last.

Therefore, my first aim should be to seek to serve God, which is the end, and only after that, if it is more profitable, to have a benefice or marry, for these are means to the end. Nothing must move me to use such means, or to deprive myself of them, save only the service and praise of God our Lord, and the salvation of my soul.

170. MATTERS ABOUT WHICH A CHOICE SHOULD BE MADE

The purpose of this consideration is to afford information on the matters about which a choice should be made. It contains four points and a note

115

FIRST POINT. It is necessary that all matters of which we wish to make a choice be either indifferent or good in themselves, and such that they are lawful within our Holy Mother, the hierarchical Church, and not bad or opposed to her.

171. SECOND POINT. There are things that fall under an unchangeable choice, such as the priesthood, marriage, etc. There are others with regard to which our choice may be changed, for example, to accept or relinquish a benefice, to receive or renounce temporal goods.

172. THIRD POINT. With regard to an unchangeable choice, once it has been made, for instance, by marriage or the priesthood, etc., since it cannot be undone, no further choice is possible. Only this is to be noted. If the choice has not been made as it should have been, and with due order, that is, if it was not made without inordinate attachments, one should be sorry for this, and take care to live well in the life he has chosen.

Since such a choice was inordinate and awry, it does not seem to be a vocation from God, as many erroneously believe. They make a divine call out of a perverse and wicked choice. For every vocation that comes from God is always pure and undefiled, uninfluenced by the flesh or any inordinate attachment.

173. FOURTH POINT. In matters that may be changed, if one has made a choice properly and with due order, without any yielding to the flesh or the world, there seems to be no reason why he should make it over. But let him perfect himself as much as possible in the one he has made.

174. *Note*

It is to be observed that if a choice in matters that are subject to change has not been made sincerely and with due order, then, if one desires to bring forth fruit that is worthwhile and most pleasing in the sight of God our Lord, it will be profitable to make a choice in the proper way.

175. THREE TIMES WHEN A CORRECT AND GOOD CHOICE OF A WAY OF LIFE MAY BE MADE

FIRST TIME. When God our Lord so moves and attracts the will that a devout soul without hesitation, or the possibility of hesitation, follows what has been manifested to it. St. Paul and St. Matthew acted thus in following Christ our Lord.

176. SECOND TIME. When much light and understanding are derived through experience of desolations and consolations and discernment of diverse spirits.

177. THIRD TIME. This is a time of tranquility. One considers first for what purpose man is born, that is, for the praise of God our Lord and for the salvation of his soul. With the desire to attain this before his mind, he chooses as a means to this end a kind of life or state within the bounds of the Church that will be a help in the service of his Lord and for the salvation of his soul.

I said it is a time of tranquility, that is, a time when the soul is not agitated by different spirits, and has free and peaceful use of its natural powers.

178. If a choice of a way of life has not been made in the first and second time, below are given:

TWO WAYS OF MAKING A CHOICE OF A WAY OF LIFE IN THE THIRD TIME

FIRST WAY OF MAKING A GOOD AND CORRECT CHOICE OF A WAY OF LIFE

SECOND WEEK

This contains six points

FIRST POINT. This is to place before my mind the object with regard to which I wish to make a choice, for example, an office, or the reception or rejection of a benefice, or anything else that may be the object of a choice subject to change.

179. SECOND POINT. It is necessary to keep as my aim the end for which I am created, that is, the praise of God our Lord and the salvation of my soul. Besides this, I must be indifferent, without any inordinate attachment, so that I am not more inclined or disposed to accept the object in question than to relinquish it, nor to give it up than to accept it. I should be like a balance at equilibrium, without leaning to either side, that I might be ready to follow whatever I perceive is more for the glory and praise of God our Lord and for the salvation of my soul.

180. THIRD POINT. I should beg God our Lord to deign to move my will, and to bring to my mind what I ought to do in this matter that would be more for His praise and glory. Then I should use the understanding to weigh the matter with care and fidelity, and make my choice in conformity with what would be more pleasing to His most holy will.

181. FOURTH POINT. This will be to weigh the matter by reckoning the number of advantages and benefits that would accrue to me if I had the proposed office or benefice solely for the praise of God our Lord and the salvation of my soul. On the other hand, I should weigh the disadvantages and dangers there might be in having it. I will do the same with the second alternative, that is, weigh the advantages and benefits as well as the disadvantages and danger of not having it.

182. FIFTH POINT. After I have gone over and pondered in this way every aspect of the matter in question, I will consider which alternative appears more reasonable. Then I must come to a decision in the matter under deliberation because of weightier motives presented to my reason, and not because of any sensual inclination.

183. SIXTH POINT. After such a choice or decision, the one who has made it must turn with great diligence to prayer in the presence of God our Lord, and offer Him his choice that the Divine Majesty may deign to accept and confirm it if it is for His greater service and praise.

184. SECOND WAY OF MAKING A CORRECT AND GOOD CHOICE OF A WAY OF LIFE

This contains four rules and a note

FIRST RULE. The love that moves and causes one to choose must descend from above, that is, from the love of God, so that before one chooses he should perceive that the greater or less attachment for the object of his choice is solely because of His Creator and Lord.

185. SECOND RULE. I should represent to myself a man whom I have never seen or known, and whom I would like to see practice all perfection. Then I should consider what I would tell him to do and choose for the greater glory of God our Lord and the greater perfection of his soul. I will do the same, and keep the rule I propose to others.

186. THIRD RULE. This is to consider what procedure and norm of action I would wish to have followed in making the present choice if I were at the moment of death. I will guide myself by this and make my decision entirely in conformity with it.

187. FOURTH RULE. Let me picture and consider myself as standing in the presence of my judge on the last day, and reflect what decision in the present matter I would then wish to have made. I will choose now the rule of life that I would then wish to have observed, that on the Day of Judgment I may be filled with happiness and joy.

188. *Note*

Guided by the rules given above for my eternal salvation and peace, I will make my decision, and will offer it to God our Lord as directed in the sixth point of the First Way of Making a Choice of a Way of Life.

189. DIRECTIONS FOR THE AMENDMENT AND REFORMATION OF ONE'S WAY OF LIVING IN ONE'S STATE OF LIFE

It must be borne in mind that some may be established in an ecclesiastical office, or may be married, and hence cannot make a choice of a state of life, or, in matters that may be changed and hence are subject to a choice, they may not be very willing to make one.

It will be very profitable for such persons, whether they possess great wealth or not, in place of a choice, to propose a way for each to reform his manner of living in his state by setting before him the purpose of his creation and of his life and position, namely, the glory and praise of God our Lord and the salvation of his soul.

If he is really to attain this end, during the exercises and during the consideration of the ways of making a choice as explained above, he will have to examine and weigh in all its details how large a household he should maintain, how he ought to rule and govern it, how he ought to teach its members by word and example. So too he should consider what part of his means should be used for his family and household, how much should be set aside for distribution to the poor and other pious purposes.

Let him desire and seek nothing except the greater praise and glory of God our Lord as the aim of all he does. For everyone must keep in mind that in all that concerns the spiritual life his progress will be in proportion to his surrender of self-love and of his own will and interests.

PRE-NOTES

Check the Act of the Presence of God

- Ask the retreatant, "Would you tell me how you are doing the Act of the Presence of God?"
- And "How is it going?"
- "What is happening when you do this and how is it making you feel?"
- The Act of the Presence of God has nothing to do with the retreatant seeing God. It is a simple reflection not on "I see God," but that right now GOD SEES ME...not that I behold God, but that "right now" God is beholding me— the retreatant. God sees me, right now.

Check the Examination of Conscience

- Ask your retreatants the same questions as above.

  ◆ "Would you tell me how you are doing the Examination of Conscience and so on?"
  ◆ "Can you walk me through how you are doing your Examination of Conscience?" And have them tell you... be intrusive.

- ◆ ...and ask them, as a physical therapist would ask you, "How do you pick up a paper from the floor? Show me."
- ◆ ...so they can see exactly what you are doing so you can correct what your motion is right there on the spot that is causing the pain.

- Call to mind as we proceed that Christ directs a person's life by the consolations and desolations of the retreat.
- Review the Second Week structure of contemplation—the five exercises: paragraphs 101–31.
- Review the grace and review the Application of the Senses here as we proceed.
- A reminder: *the retreatants' job is not to keep pace with a director's pace.*

Paragraph 169

Keep in mind that the first principle of proceeding through the Spiritual Exercises of St. Ignatius is to get a clear idea of what Ignatius means by what he is saying. Then go over paragraphs 169–89.

Paragraph 169 is an echo of the Three Classes of Persons. What is the integrating principle of this material? What is the inner unifying principle of this block of material?

- It is FREEDOM...for God to direct the life of the retreatant.
- Paragraph 169: What is this about?
    - ◆ Stimulus—response—compulsion.
    - ◆ Need—gratification.
    - ◆ Here we intersect with the motive of God.
    - ◆ God's service, God's glory, God's will between.

- Instant compulsive need intersects with gratification.
- Instant stimulus intersects with response fulfillment.

- Ignatius is looking for a FREEDOM in the retreatant so that God can enter the retreatant's life to carry out God's own designs.
- The only thing in existence that can give us freedom is the kingdom of Christ:

  ◆ The love of Christ.
  ◆ The rule of Christ.
  ◆ The will of Christ.
  ◆ The service of Christ.

- This is the only thing strong enough...powerful enough... to free us.
- St. John of the Cross in the *Living Flame of Love*: God takes something away only to give it back with a certain general freedom toward it—a gentleness to it.
- Jesus is the center of all of this:

  ◆ Jesus's life (christocentric life for us).
  ◆ Jesus's purpose.
  ◆ Jesus's will.
  ◆ Jesus's love.
  ◆ Jesus's goals.
  ◆ Jesus's kingdom.
  ◆ In the service of Jesus—the service and praise of our Divine Lord.

- The decision: What ought to be done?...What ought I to do?

Paragraph 189

What is this? God is settling out a person's life in a way that reveals an attachment of self-interest...by Christ's life...by consolations and desolations, not by MY decisions in directing.

THE THREE DEGREES OF HUMILITY: the emotion is to be with Jesus.

SECOND WEEK

How do you give the Two Standards?

- Whatever you do, do not say now is the time for you to make an election…you must make an election now as Jesus is leaving Nazareth and going to his mission—a decision: the question of generosity or mediocrity.
- Mark 6:2, *the two banquets*: Herod's banquet…interlude… and then, the *feeding of the five thousand.* Which one would you rather attend?
- Matthew14:1–12, *death of John the Baptist*—at Herod's banquet
- Matthew 15:32–39, *Jesus and the multiplication of loaves*—Jesus's banquet
- Matthew 4:11, *temptations in the desert*—baptism of Jesus versus temptations: three temptations and Jesus's responses
- Matthew 5:1–12, *the Beatitudes*
- Galatians 5, *fruits of the Spirit…fruits of sin*
- Matthew 6:24–34, *cannot serve two masters*
- Mark 10, *Sons of Zebedee*—Can you drink of the cup I will drink?
- Reflection: A question of identity…do I have riches because I am what others think of me? Do I identify myself completely with what I do, which is what pride is? Am I more than what I do?
- Deuteronomy 6, *choose death or life*
- Deuteronomy 29 and 30, *"It is in your heart"*
- Build on stages of growth. Children need affirmation and recognition, and that's okay, but do you need to grow out of that?
- How do I know which way God is leading me?
- Matthew 20:28 and Mark 10:45, Jesus's service texts: *"I have come not to be served but to serve."*

- Appeal to liturgical experiences and consciousness: use the image of voicing our baptismal promises at the Holy Saturday Easter Vigil Service: "Do you renounce Satan (and so on)?"
- 1 Kings 19, *gentle source*
- Write down on a piece of paper the ways darkness comes into your life; then write down the ways light comes into your life.
- Personally, how are you?
- How are the strategies of the Two Standards playing out in the world today?

  ◆ Affluence—prestige—power for riches—pride?
  ◆ Wisdom of God or of riches and pride?

- Fold a piece of paper and write down on one side: What is your experience of being tempted? And on the other side: What is your experience of God's grace?
- For colloquy: 1 Corinthians 1:17–25, *wisdom of God*—but to evangelize, not through the wisdom of words, lest the cross of Christ become empty....
- Psalm 33, *"All God's works are trustworthy"*

How do you give the Three Classes of People?

- Mark 10:17–27; Matthew 19:16–22; Luke 18:18–23, *the rich young man*
- Matthew 19:14, *Jesus with the children*
- Matthew 13:1–23, *the sower and the seed* parable
- Luke 16:19–31, *rich man and Lazarus*
- 2 Kings 5, *Naaman the leper*...go to the Jordan and wash seven times.
- Image of the fantasy that I won the lottery.
- It is degrees of freedom.

How do you give the Three Degrees of Love? The Three Degrees of Humility?

- It is a gift of grace to achieve the Third Degree of Humility.

  - First Degree: Behavior.
  - Second Degree: An attitude of the mind.
  - Third Degree: A desire...a feeling...out of love for Christ, I choose poverty, insults, and humiliations.

There is a deepening here, like the deepening of Exercise Three and Exercise Four of the First Week. So...

- Roleplay this: Jesus says to you, "I am equally pleased by either...riches, honors or poverty, insults." What will you do? What will you choose?...you have to choose it and to do it for you yourself alone—for you to be you: "I want to have as much in common with you as possible...as much as I possibly can...in order for me to be me—my deepest self—I want to be with Jesus: rejected, poor, insulted, wronged, abused." Paragraph 167, THE THIRD DEGREE OF HUMILITY, where the Divine Majesty would be "EQUALLY SERVED": "I would choose."
- Matthew 20:20, *mother of Zebedee's sons makes her request to Jesus*
- Philippians 3:1, I consider all as rubbish except to know Christ Jesus, and Him crucified (the Third Degree of Humility).
- Being able to go with what life presents—if it is good or bad—being able to roll and go with it (the Third Degree of Humility).
- The First Principle and Foundation is a general consideration.

- ◆ The Two Standards is delving into the particular.
  - ▪ The Two Standards can be given to concretize the retreatant's consolations and desolations.
  - ▪ The Two Standards is an outline of the dynamics of consolation and desolation.
- ◆ The movement is from the general to the particular.
- ◆ And from the general universal to the specific in my life.

How do you introduce "the treatment of choice" or a "renewal of life"?

- Remember that Christ is the progenitor of a choice here… this must be inspired by Christ.
- Remember the notion in paragraphs 155 and 169 is not to give up everything, but nothing must move me to use means or deprive myself of them…except God's inspiration (see paragraphs 179 and 181). Weigh the disadvantages and dangers of NOT HAVING IT: follow the development of this notion through these paragraphs; this goes against the misunderstood notion of Ignatian spirituality that Ignatius says that you must give up everything. This is NOT TRUE.
- So, the Examination of Conscience—how do you use it now?
- How do you give the Introduction to Making a Choice of a Way of Life material of paragraph 189…for RENEWAL?
- How do you give the confirmation in paragraphs 183 and 188?
- Why is there a confirmation sought in the Second Method only, if there are no consolations or desolations to make a decision clear?
- Concerning the confirmation: A DECISION MUST BE MADE for a confirmation to be sought.

The norms for confirmation given by St. Ignatius in his autobiography:

- The decision must have an outward priority.
- The decision must be service oriented.
- The decision must be a great good to others.
- The decision must be long lasting.

The Third and Fourth Weeks of the Spiritual Exercises are a confirmation and can confirm a decision…just keep going and Christ will confirm your decision—trust.

Ignatius's directive is to have retreatants offer their decision to God.

- The Third Week suffering and passion, pain with Christ: struggle to make the decision…is the very meaning of the Third Week of the Spiritual Exercises.
- The very meaning of the Fourth Week is victory with Christ. This gives strength and confirmation—a new joy to the decision made: this is the confirmation.
- The confirmation can also come at the Eucharist—the offertory—at the anamnesis or the Great Amen…in offering my decision to Christ at each of these eucharistic moments.
- Ask them to offer up their decisions at the offertory and these other parts of the Mass—at the anamnesis—and the doxology.
- Consider the last Rule for the Discernment of Spirits of the Second Week at these moments.

In paragraphs 135–89, St. Ignatius says to the director to be a balance—and do not exhort to poverty or no poverty.

- Why is there a confirmation sought in the Second Method: if there are no consolations or desolations to make a decision clear?
- Concerning confirmation: A DECISION MUST BE MADE for there a confirmation to be sought.
- The norms for confirmation given by St. Ignatius in his autobiography:

  ◆ The decision must have an outward priority.
  ◆ The decision must be service oriented.
  ◆ The decision must be a great good to others.
  ◆ The decision must be long lasting.

- Get clear what St. Ignatius is saying.
- Paragraph 135: Introduction to the Different States of Life

What will set this off?

The grace of Ignatian contemplation—from some episode in the life of Christ—Christ chooses the episode and what to make a choice about: THIS IS WHAT I HAVE BEEN CHOSEN FOR...CHOSEN BY CHRIST.

What does "the enemy of our human nature" mean?

THE TWO STANDARDS

As Introduction to a Consideration of Different States of Life:

- What will set this off? The grace of Ignatian contemplation...from some episode in the life of Christ. Christ chooses the episode and what to make a choice about: THIS IS WHAT I HAVE BEEN CHOSEN FOR...CHOSEN BY CHRIST....
- What does "the enemy of our human nature" mean?

The Two Standards: as an Introduction to Considering Different States of Life:

- How sin works—how grace works.
- This is a tool to make me more sensitive so I can listen to what Christ is moving me to.
- Look at the VERBS in this meditation.
- The Two Standards is not about a choice between Jesus and Satan, but about means and strategies. It is about knowledge…the gift of knowledge of the strategies of Satan and the knowledge of the strategies of Jesus: the "ways" of each.

Knowledge of the deceits of Satan:

- Riches: What kind of riches? Yes…
- Binds a person by coveting riches.
- If you go for riches, honors, and pride, you get to the top and it's pretty empty because that's all you get—riches, honors, pride.

Knowledge of the true-life example of Christ:

- An updated meaning of pride: I'm the center of all, the source of all. As in, "I'm in charge of the retreat."

  ◆ Christ's example is of poverty, insults, and humiliation.

- An updated meaning of humility: God is the center of all, and I receive gifts from God.

  ◆ For example: the sun revolves around the earth versus heliocentricity, where the earth revolves around the sun—a totally different and new worldview.

Paragraph 136—on the fourth day—the Two Standards is done four times with the Three Classes of Persons as the Fifth Exercise, as a Repetition.

Paragraph 148 notes,

- The first at midnight.
- The second in the morning.
- The third repetition.
- The fourth repetition.
- The fifth, the Three Classes of Persons, paragraph 149: The Triple Colloquy.

Meditation: The Three Classes of Persons

- The Three Classes of Persons is like the First Exercise of the First Week in that it starts with "sin...out there... objective...out there in the world...away from me." Then it moves inward to "my sinfulness." Likewise, the Three Classes is a situation "out there" away from me, and then in the Second Week the movement is into within me and my reform or choice, personal to me, moving inward to me.
- To become free of the burden—the burden of the attachment (paragraph 150)
- The Three Classes is an inner test of the quality of freedom the retreatant has.
- They want not to be controlled by what they have...so that money is not the primary concern of their lives.
- This is a purification because all that I have, I have with impure motivations.
- First Class: PROCRASTINATORS...approach... WISHERS.
- Second Class: COMPROMISERS...approach... TALKERS.
- Third Class: DOERS...in freedom, approach...an exercise to set in shape in order to have Christ pick something for me to do...for Christ to live his life in me...**to will as Christ inspires me to will and to do.**
- Paragraph 155: FREEDOM...The Third Class.

The Fifth Day: Contemplation of Jesus leaving Nazareth, paragraph 158

This is done five times:

- Paragraph 164 is the same day: the Three Degrees of Humility is a consideration. Think it over, reviewing paragraphs 165, 166, and 167. This is really the Three Degrees of Love; that is, the three kinds of love, as the humility spoken of here is a consequence of love of Christ.

  - ◆ It follows from love of the person of Christ…wanting to be with Him…wanting to be identified with Him… wanting to imitate Him.
  - ◆ It is a deepening of the Three Classes of Persons, so giving this is really meant to be done in the third and fourth repetition of the fifth day.
  - ◆ It is going to the Jordan…leaving home…because the third and fourth repetitions are for "deepening" the graces—consolations and desolations.

- Paragraph 163: the choice of a way of life requires gaining information for a decision.
- Paragraph 189: involves reformation and surrender of will and intellect.
- Fold all into the Examination of Conscience—Why? To let the grace live and breathe moment by moment.

The Three Classes of Persons—a repetition of the Two Standards

This is all happening on the fifth day because Jesus is leaving Nazareth and going to have an experience at the Jordan River.

This is

- Jesus's touchstone experience.
- Jesus's experience of mission.
- Jesus's experience of vocation.
- Jesus's choice…a mobile lifestyle.
- A state of life.
- An affirmation: "You are My Son" (Luke 3:21–22).
- Jesus's public life.

With the Three Degrees of Humility and the Three Degrees of Love, desire and love come together:

- Law orientation…no mortal sin.
- Service wants more closeness, indifference…no venial sin.
- Will and likeness…a climate of desire.

Thomas Green, SJ, wrote about hating to go to the hospital, but his mother was there, dying, and therefore, he loved the hospital after she died because she was there. It is the same with Christ—Christ had it, therefore, I want it…I love humiliations because Christ had them.

In another example, a nun who had cancer went into remission, and she said, "I miss it (cancer) because I was in union with Christ's suffering, and the bond I had with Him was so deep."

Chapter 10

THE RULES FOR THE DISCERNMENT OF SPIRITS OF THE SECOND WEEK OF THE SPIRITUAL EXERCISES

From the text of the Spiritual Exercises of St. Ignatius of Loyola:

328. RULES FOR DISCERNMENT OF SPIRITS

Further rules for understanding the different movements produced in the soul. They serve for a more accurate discernment of spirits and are more suitable for the second week
329. 1. It is characteristic of God and His Angels, when they act upon the soul, to give true happiness and spiritual joy, and to banish all the sadness and disturbances which are caused by the enemy.

It is characteristic of the evil one to fight against such happiness and consolation by proposing fallacious reasonings, subtitles, and continual deceptions.

330. 2. God alone can give consolation to the soul without any previous cause. It belongs solely to the Creator to come into a

soul, to leave it, to act upon it, to draw it wholly to the love of His Divine Majesty. I said without previous cause, that is, without any preceding perception or knowledge of any subject by which a soul might be led to such a consolation through its own acts of intellect and will.

331. 3. If a cause precedes, both the good angel and the evil spirit can give consolation to a soul, but for a quite different purpose. The good angel consoles for the progress of the soul, that it may advance and rise to what is more perfect. The evil spirit consoles for purposes that are the contrary, and that afterwards he might draw the soul to his own perverse intentions and wickedness.

332. 4. It is a mark of the evil spirit to assume the appearance of an angel of light. He begins by suggesting thoughts that are suited to a devout soul, and ends by suggesting his own. For example, he will suggest holy and pious thoughts that are wholly in conformity with the sanctity of the soul. Afterwards, he will endeavor little by little to end by drawing the soul into his hidden snares and evil designs.

333. 5. We must carefully observe the whole course of our thoughts. If the beginning and middle and end of the course of thoughts are wholly good and directed to what is entirely right, it is a sign that they are from the good angel. But the course of thoughts suggested to us may terminate in something evil, or distracting, or less good than the soul had formerly proposed to do. Again, it may end in what weakens the soul, or disquiets it; or by destroying the peace, tranquility, and quiet which it had before, it may cause disturbance to the soul. These things are a clear sign that the thoughts are proceeding from the evil spirit, the enemy of our progress and eternal salvation.

334. 6. When the enemy of our human nature has been detected and recognized by the trail of evil marking his course and by the wicked end to which he leads us, it will be profitable for one who has been tempted to review immediately the whole course of the temptation. Let him consider the series of good thoughts, how they arose, how the evil one gradually attempted to make him step down from the state of spiritual delight and joy in which he was, till finally he drew him to his wicked designs. The purpose of this review is that once such an experience has been understood and carefully observed, we may guard ourselves for the future against the customary deceits of the enemy.

335. 7. In souls that are progressing to greater perfection, the action of the good angel is delicate, gentle, delightful. It may be compared to a drop of water penetrating a sponge.

The action of the evil spirit upon such souls is violent, noisy, and disturbing. It may be compared to a drop of water falling upon a stone.

In souls that are going from bad to worse, the action of the spirits mentioned above is just the reverse. The reason for this is to be sought in the opposition or similarity of these souls to the different kinds of spirits. When the disposition is contrary to that of the spirits, they enter with noise and commotion that are easily perceived. When the disposition is similar to that of the spirits, they enter silently, as one coming into his own house when the doors are open.

336. 8. When consolation is without previous cause, as was said, there can be no deception in it, since it can proceed from God our Lord only. But a spiritual person who has received such a consolation must consider it very attentively, and must cautiously distinguish the actual time of the consolation from the period which follows it. At such a time the soul is

still fervent and favored with the grace and after effects of the consolation which has passed. In this second period the soul frequently forms various resolutions and plans which are not granted directly by God our Lord. They may come from our own reasoning on the relations of our concepts and on the consequences of our judgments, or they may come from the good or evil spirit. Hence, they must be carefully examined before they are given full approval and put into execution.

337. RULES FOR THE DISTRIBUTION OF ALMS

In the ministry of distributing alms the following rules should be observed

338. 1. If I distribute alms to my relatives or friends or persons to whom I am attached, there are four things that must be considered. Some of these were mentioned in treating the Choice of a Way of Life.

The first is that the love that moves me and causes me to give the alms must be from above, that is, from the love of God our Lord. Hence, I should be conscious within myself that God is the motive of the greater or less love that I bear toward these persons, and that God is manifestly the cause of my loving them more.

339. 2. I should place before my mind a person whom I have never seen or known, and whom I wish to be wholly perfect in the office and state of life which he occupies. Now the same standard of action that I would like him to follow in his way of distributing alms for the greater glory of God and the perfection of his soul I myself will observe, and do neither more nor less. The same rule I would like him to follow, and the norm I judge would be for the glory of God I shall abide by myself.

340. 3. I should picture myself at the hour of my death, and ponder well the way and norm I would then wish to have observed in carrying out the duties of my office. I will lay down the same rule for myself now, and keep it in my distribution of alms.

341. 4. I should imagine myself before my judge on the last day, and weigh well the manner in which I would wish then to have done my duty in carrying out this office. The same rule that I would then wish to have observed I will keep now.

342. 5. When one finds that he is inclined or attached to some persons to whom he wishes to give alms, let him stop and ponder well the four rules given above. He must investigate and test his affection by them. He should not give the alms until in conformity with these rules he has completely put off and cast aside his inordinate attachment.

343. 6. It is true that there is no wrong in receiving the goods of God our Lord for distribution if a person is called by God our Lord to such a service. Nevertheless, there may be question of a fault and excess in the amount he retains and applies to his own needs of what he holds to give to others. Hence one can reform his way of living in his state by the rules given above.

344. 7. For these and many other reasons it will always be better and safer in all matters concerning himself and his household, if one is saving and cuts down expenses as much as possible, if he imitates as closely as he can our great High Priest, model, and guide, Christ our Lord.

It was in conformity with this doctrine that the Third Council of Carthage, at which St. Augustine was present, decided and decreed that the furniture of the bishop should be cheap and poor.

The same consideration applies to all stations in life, but attention must be given to adapting it to each one's condition and rank.

In matrimony we have the example of St. Joachim and St. Anne. They divided their resources into three parts. The first they gave to the poor. The second they donated to the ministrations and services of the Temple. The third they used for the support of themselves and their household.

THE FIFTH DAY OF THE SECOND WEEK OF THE SPIRITUAL EXERCISES

Paragraph 328, Rules for the Discernment of Spirits for the Second Week

- First Week rules focus on self: the problem could be that a retreatant has a bad self-image (or self-concept).
- Second Week rules focus on Christ—a contemplation of God. So the problem could be that a retreatant has a bad image of God—an erroneous concept of God.

Pre-Note 1

I bring this up because one of the obvious problems about all of the Second Week material is that the Second Week is hampered if I feel that God is "out to get me," resulting in a fear of being punished by God. This results in a fear of giving God my life.

Fear of giving God

- Control.
- Authority, as a retreatant could have problems with authority.
- Obedience...can be a bad word to some from bad experiences in the past.

- Openness that could affect choices—being open and trusting of God or not.

The issue of "control" applies to you as a director as well, for if you "bracket and put on the shelf" the retreatants' "decision of why they came" and let them have free range through the Galilean ministry of Jesus to contemplate...you as a director don't know what will happen. Can you let go of control of your retreatants?

Pre-Note 2

A problem that we are familiar with:

- Development of the image of God in the history of Israel in the Old Testament from: a God of war and punishment to a God of Love—Jesus—in the New Testament. This change caused Jesus a lot of problems regarding religion, and the people as well.
- One's concept of God can change.
- The Second Week can involve a change in the concept of God of a retreatant initiated by God in the contemplation of Jesus.
- Do you have the courage to let go of control as a director of the Spiritual Exercises?
- Put the control of the retreatants in Christ's hands—the sole control of what will happen to your retreatants in the hands of their Creator and Lord. Can you abandon your retreatants to Christ and let go of what you as a director of the Spiritual Exercises think should happen?
- Can you as a director take the tension of not knowing what is going to happen to your retreatants...letting the retreatants free range through the Gospel accounts of Jesus to find their way to Him?

Pre-Note 3

STEP I

Rules for the Discernment of the Second Week: Paragraph 328

Why are these Rules for the Second Week?

- Good people are tempted by the good.
- A decision can be between one good and another good.
- A decision can be between one good and a better good.
- There is something more in St. Ignatius's life than his generosity; it is the power and movement of the love and will of God…this is what we are looking for. It is more important than a retreatant moving with enthusiasm—a quality of generosity that in six months won't even be remembered and will lead to castigation and disappointment for not having it.
- We are not looking in the Second Week for ephemeral human enthusiasm, but one is looking for the lasting imprint of the love and the will of God. For this, one has to learn to wait for it.

STEP II

What are the signs within the retreatant that are asking you to give them the Rules for the Discernment of Spirits of the Second Week?

The grace of the Second Week of the Spiritual Exercises:

- It is better to err on "while contemplating the life of Christ" treatment so that the Two Standards, the Three Classes of Persons, the Three Degrees of Humility are a disposition of begging Christ to give them the disposition.

- So, it is not a choosing on the part of the retreatants but a being chosen by God that we are asking for and looking to receive.

STEP III

How do you give and use the Rules of Discernment of Spirits of the Second Week?

- What arises are choices between goods.
- How do you use these rules with the material concerning a choice?
- How do you use the Examination of Conscience in all of this material?

  - The gift one is looking for is to answer: "Where is God?"
  - What is the nature of the interfacing between the Examination of Conscience the Rules for the Discernment of Spirits of the Second Week, the material of a way for Making a Choice, and the gift of Ignatian contemplation of the Second Week of the Spiritual Exercises?

- There is a CONFLUENCE here of these four rivers—these distinct elements go to make up the art of spiritual direction within the context of giving the Spiritual Exercises.

  - Throughout this confluence, these distinct elements must remain distinct as we proceed.
  - We need to distinguish these themes—these thematics—as we proceed here, in order to come to an integrity of effect.
  - They all move toward a sensitivity to Christ.
  - They mutually inform each other toward purity of intention in seeking to be with Christ.

- What is happening in you as a person now?

  - What is happening in you as a devotion now?
  - How is it making you feel?
  - What is happening in your prayer now? How is it making you feel?
  - What is happening in your direction now? How is it making you feel?

- How are you giving the Second Week contemplations of the Spiritual Exercises? Are the retreatants being given "permission" to "free range" along the Gospels to pick which scene in the life of Christ to contemplate?

The question begins to arise as to how you are giving the material of the choice of a way of life, a choice of different states of life.

- How are you giving the Rules for the Discernment of Spirits?
- How are you giving the Examination of Conscience?
- How are these interfacing now?
- What about the retreatants who have a bad image of God?
- How is Christ selecting a choice or a reformation of life issue in the prayer of your retreatants?
- How is Christ taking over as retreat director of the retreat now?
- What is the grace of the Third Week of the Spiritual Exercises?

THIRD WEEK

Chapter 11

THE GRACE AND PROCEDURE OF THE THIRD WEEK OF THE SPIRITUAL EXERCISES

From the text of the Spiritual Exercises of St. Ignatius of Loyola:

190. FIRST DAY. THE FIRST CONTEMPLATION AT MIDNIGHT

Christ our Lord goes from Bethany to Jerusalem and the Last Supper.

289. It contains the preparatory prayer, three preludes, six points, and a colloquy.

PRAYER. The usual preparatory prayer.

191. FIRST PRELUDE. This is the history. Here it will be to recall that Christ our Lord sent two of His disciples from Bethany to Jerusalem to prepare the Supper, and afterwards, He Himself went there with His disciples. After they had eaten the Paschal

Lamb and supped, He washed their feet, and gave His most Sacred Body and Precious Blood to His disciples. When Judas had gone out to sell his Lord, Christ addressed His disciples.

192. SECOND PRELUDE. This is a mental representation of the place. Here it will be to consider the way from Bethany to Jerusalem, whether narrow or broad, whether level, etc.; also the place of the Supper, whether great or small, whether of this or that appearance.

193. THIRD PRELUDE. This is to ask for what I desire. Here it will be to ask for sorrow, compassion, and shame because the Lord is going to His suffering for my sins.

194. FIRST POINT. This is to see the persons at the Supper, and to reflect upon myself, and strive to draw some profit from them.

SECOND POINT. This is to listen to their conversation, and likewise seek to draw fruit from it.

THIRD POINT. This is to see what they are doing, and to seek to draw some fruit from it.

195. FOURTH POINT. This will be to consider what Christ our Lord suffers in His human nature, or according to the passage contemplated, what he desires to suffer. Then I will begin with great effort to strive to grieve, be sad, and weep. In this way I will labor through all the points that follow.

196. FIFTH POINT. This is to consider how the divinity hides itself; for example, it could destroy its enemies and does not do so, but leaves the most sacred humanity to suffer so cruelly.

197. SIXTH POINT. This is to consider that Christ suffers all this for my sins, and what I ought to do and suffer for Him.

198. COLLOQUY. Close with a colloquy to Christ our Lord, and at the end, say the *Our Father*.

199. *Note*

Attention must be called to the following point which was mentioned before and in part explained. In the colloquy, one should talk over motives and present petitions according to circumstances. Thus he may be tempted or he may enjoy consolation, may desire to have this virtue or another, may want to dispose himself in this or that way, may seek to grieve or rejoice according to the matter that he is contemplating. Finally, he should ask what he more earnestly desires with regard to some particular interests.

Following this advice, he may engage in only one colloquy with Christ our Lord, or, if the matter and his devotion prompt him to do so, he may use three colloquies, one with the Mother of our Lord, one with her Son, and one with the Father. If three colloquies are used, the same form should be followed that was given in the meditation on Two Standards, and the note that follows after the Three Classes of Men should be observed.

200. SECOND CONTEMPLATION

In the morning. From the Last Supper to the Agony in the Garden inclusive

PRAYER. The usual preparatory prayer.

201. FIRST PRELUDE. This is the history of the mystery. Here it will be as follows: Christ our Lord descended with the eleven disciples from Mt. Sion, where the Supper was held, to the Valley

of Josaphat. Eight of the disciples were left at a place in the valley, and the other three in a part of the garden. Then Jesus began His prayer, and His sweat became as drops of blood. Three times He prayed to His Father and went to rouse His disciples from sleep. After His enemies had fallen to the ground at His word, and Judas had given Him the kiss, after St. Peter had cut off the ear of Malchus, and Christ had healed it, Jesus was seized as a malefactor, and led down through the valley and again up the slope to the house of Annas.

202. SECOND PRELUDE. This is to see the place. It will be here to consider the way from Mt. Sion to the Valley of Josaphat, likewise the garden, its breadth, its length, and appearance.

203. THIRD PRELUDE. This is to ask for what I desire. In the Passion it is proper to ask for sorrow with Christ in sorrow, anguish with Christ in anguish, tears and deep grief because of the great affliction Christ endures for me.

NOTES

204. NOTE I. In this second contemplation, after the preparatory prayer and the three preludes given above, the same way of proceeding in the points and colloquies is to be observed as was followed in the first contemplation on the Supper.

About the time of Mass and Vespers, two repetitions are to be made of the first and second contemplations. Before supper the Application of the Senses should be made on the subject matter of the two contemplations. The preparatory prayer, and the preludes, adapted to the subject of the exercise, are always to precede. The form to be observed is the same as that given and explained in the Second Week.

205. NOTE II. As far as age, health, and physical constitution permit the exercitant to do so, he will use five exercises each day, or fewer.

206. NOTE III. In the Third Week some modification of the second and sixth Additional Directions is necessary.

The second will be that as soon as I awake, I will mind where I am going and the purpose. I will briefly summarize the contemplation on which I am about to enter. According to the subject matter, I will make an effort while rising and dressing to be sad and grieve because of the great sorrow and suffering of Christ our Lord.

The sixth Additional Direction will be changed as follows. I will take care not to bring up pleasing thoughts, even though they are good and holy, for example, of the Resurrection and the glory of heaven. Rather I will rouse myself to sorrow, suffering, and anguish by frequently calling to mind the labors, fatigue, and suffering which Christ our Lord endured from the time of His birth down to the mystery of the passion upon which I am engaged at present.

207. NOTE IV. The Particular Examination of Conscience should be made on the exercises and the Additional Directions as applied to this Week, as was done in the past Week.

208. SECOND DAY

At midnight, the contemplation will be on the events from the Garden to the house of Annas inclusive. Cf. # 291.

In the morning, from the house of Annas to the house of Caiphas inclusive. Cf. # 292.

There will be two repetitions and the Application of the Senses as explained above.

THIRD WEEK

THIRD DAY

At midnight, from the house of Caiphas to the house of Pilate inclusive. Cf. # 293.

In the morning, from Pilate to Herod inclusive. Cf. # 294.

Then the repetitions and the Application of the Senses in the same way as has been noted.

FOURTH DAY

At midnight, from Herod to Pilate, # 295, using for this contemplation only the first half of what occurred in the house of Pilate, and afterwards in the morning, the remaining part.

There will be the two repetitions and the Application of the Senses as explained.

FIFTH DAY

At midnight, from the house of Pilate to the Crucifixion, # 296, and in the morning, from the raising of the cross to His death, # 297.

Thereafter the repetitions and the Application of the Senses.

SIXTH DAY

At midnight from the taking down from the cross to the burial exclusive, # 298, and in the morning from the burial inclusive to the house to which our Lady retired after the burial of her Son.

SEVENTH DAY

The contemplation of the whole passion in one exercise at midnight, and again in the morning.

In place of the two repetitions and the Application of the Senses, one should consider as frequently as possible throughout this whole day that the most Sacred Body of Christ our Lord remained separated from the soul, and the place and manner of burial. Let him consider, likewise, the desolation of our Lady, her great sorrow and weariness, and also that of the disciples.

209. *Note*

If one wishes to spend more time on the passion, he should use fewer mysteries in each contemplation, thus, in the first, only the Supper; in the second, only the washing of feet; in the third, the institution of the Blessed Sacrament; in the fourth, Christ's parting address, and so on for the other contemplations and mysteries.

In like manner, after the passion is finished, he may devote one whole day to the consideration of the first half of the passion, and a second day to the other half, and a third day to the whole passion.

On the other hand, if he should wish to spend less time on the passion, he may take the Supper at midnight, the Agony in the Garden in the morning; about the time of Mass, Jesus before Annas; about the time of Vespers, Jesus before Caiphas; and instead of the Application of the Senses at the hour before supper, Jesus before Pilate. In this way, without repetitions or Applications of the Senses, there should be five exercises each day, using for each one a distinct mystery of the life of Christ our Lord. After he has finished the whole passion in this way, he may use another day to go through the entire passion, either in one exercise or in several, as is deemed best for his greater profit.

INTRODUCTION TO THE THIRD WEEK OF THE SPIRITUAL EXERCISES OF ST. IGNATIUS OF LOYOLA

Two months after the retreat is over, are the retreatants going to have a director with them in their prayer? They are going to have only their Creator and Lord with them in their prayer two months from now. Maybe and maybe not...what is important is to ensure that their Creator and Lord is their only Director in this thirty-day retreat, because in two months in their prayer, they will only have with them their Creator and Lord, and may not have a spiritual director.

STEP I

What is the grace and gift of the Third Week of the Spiritual Exercises...the movement...the experience...the gift...and the "work" of the Third Week of the Spiritual Exercises?

- The first contemplation at midnight: paragraph 193, sorrow, compassion, shame because God is going to his suffering for my sins.
- The second contemplation in the morning: paragraph 203, sorrow with Christ in sorrow. Anguish with Christ in anguish. Tears and deep grief because of the deep affliction Christ endures for me.
- What is the relationship between the third prelude of the first exercise (paragraph 193) and the third prelude of the second exercise (paragraph 203)?
- Paragraph 193: the emphasis is on the retreatants being in pain and sorrow because of the retreatants' sins causing Christ pain.
- The shame of paragraph 193: we stand responsible for sending Christ to His cross...Christ deserves so much better from me...of me.
- The grace of paragraph 203: an intimate compassion for Christ.
- The emphasis here is on Christ being in pain—the emphasis is on Christ.
- The grace is being more caught up in Christ.

- It is centering more on Christ—a compassionate centering on the Person of Christ in pain.
- It is important to check the retreatants on where the pain and sorrow is coming from and track that.
- Reverse this by compassion FOR Christ…as Veronica with the role of ministering to Christ.
- The grace of the Application of the Senses prayer is SENTIR: "I FEEL IT IN MY BONES"—A FELT THOUGHT—a unity of thought, feeling, and spirit.
- When retreatants console Christ on the cross, Christ turns to each retreatant and says, "I'm with you in your carrying your cross for Me," and this allows and leads the retreatant into their own pain to suffer. This grace is not coming from the retreatant.

DIMENSIONS OF THE MOVEMENT FROM PARAGRAPHS 193 TO 203

- There is a movement from paragraph 193 to paragraph 203, from the focus on the retreatant to a focus on Christ.
- Paragraphs 193 and 203 are in the present tense, not the past tense. It is Christ suffering His passion NOW—in the now—and our compassion is NOW…in the NOW for Christ suffering NOW.
- These next three points should go in the Step III section as well:

  ◆ You feel the suffering of Christ;
  ◆ Points 1, 2, and 3 are an application of the senses;
  ◆ Points 4, 5, and 6 are almost a meditation: "consider… consider."

- Paragraph 194: Ignatius frontloads the Application of the Senses into the first exercise: he expects a facility with Application of the Senses prayer.

- Paragraph 199: Isn't it consoling when someone understands you in your suffering? Yes! Isn't this the grace of the
Third Week (in reverse), where Christ consoles me in my
suffering…mostly in the retreatant's past life, as where the
retreatant's past comes up in the Third Week. This is the
same material as in the First Week, but deeper and an "I'm
not alone" experience—isn't this the grace of the Third
Week? We are filling up the sufferings of Christ so that
our own suffering becomes MEANINGFUL: the grace of
the Application of the Senses prayer is MEANING. Is it a
surprise I can't get away from my own suffering as I look at
Jesus? Isn't this the grace of Ignatian contemplation?
- The retreatants learn the cost of discipleship by walking
with the Lord, as Christ touches the deepest parts of their
fidelity and love. The retreatants suffer with Him, not
because suffering is good, but because fidelity to one's love
is all we have.

  - There is the intimacy of being with someone suffering.
  - It matters to Jesus that I'm with Him in His suffering…
  it's an honor.

- Pray the Third Week with people around Jesus.
- Life changes a person. At eighteen, the passion can be difficult, but at sixty—"I need the passion."
- The grace of accompanying Jesus in His powerlessness…
someone innocent here is suffering.

  - This is offered by God when I'm ready, and when God
  is ready.
  - There is a quality of attentiveness…to Jesus…and to
  everyone. This grace is offered to "long-term adults."
  - This grace is when our own passion of the now begins
  to come up as we console Jesus on the cross: the
  retreatants realize that the passion of Jesus is a NOW

event—in one's own world—in one's own brothers and sisters and in oneself NOW.

- Here...retreatants need to get their eyes off their own sinfulness and to get them more and more absorbed on Christ suffering for them—this is the PROGRESSION OF THIS GRACE.

  - As this happens, the retreatants develop a compassion for Christ in His suffering on the cross.
  - As this happens, retreatants start to CONSOLE CHRIST ON THE CROSS...AS VERONICA DID then.
  - As this happens CHRIST BEGINS TO CONSOLE THE RETREATANTS in the retreatants' passion in their life in the twenty-first century and from the beginning of their suffering—perhaps the last fifty years or their whole lifetime.
  - AS THIS HAPPENS, RETREATANTS ARE BEGINNING TO FEEL THAT Jesus is their lifetime Friend... an intimate Friend, because Jesus has experienced exactly what the retreatants have experienced...being abused...not recognized as valuable...rejected; and the retreatants confide in Jesus as an equal Friend.
  - As this happens, Jesus's realistic friendship extended from the cross allows the retreatants to enter into the passion of their own lives and suffer it—the pain the retreatants may have resisted all their life.
  - As this happens the retreatants can see the passion that all of the world is in NOW as the Passion of Christ NOW. As St. Paul says, "We are filling up the sufferings of Christ" NOW...(Col 1:23–25).

- And the retreatants can welcome in all of the suffering of the world NOW, identifying it with Christ.

- This is NOT coming from the retreatants looking at themselves…it is ministered by Christ to the retreatants from the cross as the retreatants keep their eyes on Christ on the cross.
- Christ is saying to the retreatants, "I AM with you"… this allows retreatants to suffer their own pain and the pain of our sisters and brothers in the world: IT GIVES MEANING. This is the grace of an Application of the Senses prayer: this is SENTIR.

STEP II

- What are the signs that one is ready and asking for the Third Week of the Spiritual Exercises?
- When the Two Standards moves from a meditation to a contemplation—head to heart, head into the retreatants' inside—the passion is being lived out as the Two Standards: as in the life of Christ, and it is the same for the retreatant.
- When I choose the Third Degree of Humility because Christ does…BUT…I know that I'm unable to do it myself…I NEED CHRIST TO GO TO HIS PASSION FOR ME TO DO IT.
- Growing ability to use the Application of the Senses prayer.
- An abiding sense of peace, calm, and eagerness to contemplate Christ in his passion.
- A being attracted to and taken up in the Two Standards and the Three Degrees of Humility.
- There is a closure of election or reformation of life process: one completes the election process or finishes the reformation of life process…with a confirmation…and NOW… IN ORDER TO LIVE IT OUT I NEED THE PASSION…I NEED CHRIST TO GO TO HIS PASSION FOR ME.
- A desire to be with Jesus as He walks toward Jerusalem.

- A dryness—the passion—you are already in it if dryness perdures, or a perduring sorrow: Jesus is forging His passion in the retreatant.
- A need to contemplate Christ on the cross to get the Third Degree of Humility.
- A sense of gratitude for Christ going to the cross.
- Christ brought up such and such a thing—evil—in my life. Now He is going after the evil in my life and all evil on the cross.
- Jesus's demand of suffering of me, yet there is a joy in it and there is a peace in it.
- A sense of the meaning: "it will cost me"—a sense of the cost.
- This is the gift of Application of the Senses prayer.
- When retreatants console Jesus in his suffering, they experience joy.
- The retreatants want to carry their own cross.
- Retreatants start talking about an episode of the Third Week of the Spiritual Exercises, such as the agony in the Garden.
- When the retreatants are aware of what their sins have done to Jesus.

  ◆ "I have come to the end of the line. I can't struggle any more...against evil." They need the Third Week material and grace to do it for them. "All I've done does not work...give me the strength of Christ"...in the Third Week of the Spiritual Exercises.
  ◆ This same dynamic applies in other dimensions at work here; for example, making an election for a state of life or a reformation of life, meaning "I can't make the reformation of life I want to make...I need the strength of Christ in His Passion to do it—to decide to do it."

- My task is done, now it must be Christ's work…His strength.
- A sense of being a companion of Jesus as He goes to His cross.
- An awareness of the cost of discipleship—the retreatants are taking that seriously.
- The retreatants say, "I wonder what kind of pain Christ suffered? Did He suffer what I'm suffering?"
- A move from being an outside spectator in contemplation to Jesus and I being together—"I'm with Him"—I want to be with Him.

  - Love of the Eucharist comes up: the retreatants are drawn to a love of the Eucharist.
  - A deeper desire to know how Jesus loves me is present (even in my suffering).
  - A deeper desire to know how Jesus loves me even in my suffering is present.
  - An appropriation takes place in the retreatants of a felt knowledge that they are companions of Jesus.

- If the retreatants say something along these lines: "I know where this is going…this is going into pain" (on Calvary), but I "must go with Him"…"I must be with Him now"… "I cannot abandon Him now"…There is a "musting" to be with Jesus in his suffering.
- Their own weakness to do the colloquy of the Two Standards or the Third Class of Persons or the Third Degree of Humility—the retreatants can't give themselves the strength.
- A terrible personal life experience of fear or tragedy or evil comes back to some retreatants as tangible and experiential—they are reliving it as it happened to Jesus and then to them.

- Christ deeply desires to die so that He may be present to us all in this new way, as St. John Chrysostom says: "Those we love and lose are no longer where they were before. They are now wherever we are." "It is better for you that I go, because then I can send you the Holy Spirit (My Spirit)" (cf. John 16:7).
- A DEEPENING CLOSNESS TO Jesus.

  - ◆ Being attracted to the stations of the cross...inside or outside of formal prayer times.
  - ◆ Getting caught up in the momentum of Jesus moving toward his passion.
  - ◆ A growing sense "I can't do this myself"...a growing consistency of this.
  - ◆ A readiness to welcome the grace of tears.

- THE COST OF THIS is the fulfillment of my life—the meaning of my life. There is a joy in it. The "meaning" here is the meaning that comes as the gift of the Application of the Senses prayer—all sense data results in a sense of meaning.
- "To pay the COST is the joy of my life."
- If you have a sense that the retreatants are ready for the Third Week and you ask them if they are, and they say, "I'm ready (with enthusiasm)...this is what I want to do," the enthusiasm tells you that they are ready.
- MOVE PEOPLE WHEN THEY HAVE THE SIGNS.

  - ◆ The retreatants are encountering and contemplating Jesus's confrontations with the Scribes and Pharisees...or...Jesus's predictions of His passion. And the retreatants are saying, "There's more involved here... there is a cost of discipleship (suffering) involved. I don't want that suffering but I must go with Jesus as He enters this suffering, even though I don't want to...or I do want to."

- ◆ The immensity of my inability to forgive: I need Christ to go to His passion for me to do it.
- ◆ A deep sense that I am powerless.
- ◆ A disposition of intimacy with Christ as a prayer ability and facility: this is already Third Week prayer... an Application of the Senses prayer disposition, which itself is a sign a person is ready for the Third Week.
- ◆ I realize the cost of discipleship...I'm ready for the Third Week—this is a sign.

- Move people when they have the signs.

  - ◆ I need You, Lord, to go to Your passion on the cross and conquer evil forever and for me in my life because I'm unable to conquer evil in my life—in myself—and in the world. I don't have the strength.
  - ◆ I'm praying for You, Lord (rooting for You...like in sports or the Olympics, for a U.S. swimmer to win the gold.)
  - ◆ I'm praying for You, Lord, to conquer all evil on the cross, as I need you to do it FOR ME now as I'm unable to do it. I don't have the strength to do it in my life, Lord. I need You to do it on the cross for me—Help me, Lord—begging...supporting Christ...rooting for Him to do it for me—for me in my problems and needs.
  - ◆ Please do not let me sin. Keep me from entering into evil ways, a sinful life. Save me!

STEP III

How does St. Ignatius give the Third Week of the Spiritual Exercises?

Paragraph 204: Same as the Second Week.
Paragraph 209: More days...seven days in the Third Week... perhaps more...perhaps less.

Paragraph 194: Ignatius frontloads the Application of the Senses prayer method into the First Exercise: he expects a facility with the Application of the Senses prayer.

In the First Exercise you feel the suffering: points 1, 2, and 3 are an Application of the Senses.

Chapter 12

ON GIVING THE THIRD WEEK OF THE SPIRITUAL EXERCISES

HOW DO YOU GIVE THE THIRD WEEK?

Let us look at how the four Gospel evangelists give the Third Week of the Spiritual Exercises. The passion narratives of Matthew—Mark—Luke—John: How do you use these?

- The original Gospel was "the passion narrative"; then the rest of the Gospel came and was written and filled in.
- Full Gospels were written after AD 70.

  - The Gospels were written from the question, "Who is responsible for the death of Jesus?" The Jews and the Romans are symbols of us.
  - The passion narratives are four distinct theologies and very different stories.
  - See the Gospel parallels.

- Ignatius approached the passion narrative from the point of view of the hymn in Philippians and in 1 Corinthians, at the ends of chapter 1 and chapter 2...the scandal of the cross.

- Ray Brown subscribes to the following: there are skeletal facts of the passion with different theological overlays and different theological reflections of early church communities.
- Which of the four passion narratives is more accurate?
- Which of the four passion narratives is "better"? These two questions are not applicable. One is NOT BETTER than the other.
- It is a theological drama told four ways.
- Each tells the religious significance of the death of Jesus.
- Each of these four passion narratives has its own theology for a specific problem in a specific historical community. They wrote it for that context. HOW ABOUT NOW? Isn't it the same? For us directors? And retreatants?
- The question is which passion narrative is best for a retreatant?—for a specific retreatant NOW with a specific issue...path...or problem?
- Remember one thing about how the Gospels, and, in particular, the Gospel passion narratives were written: **the further you get away from your parents' death (or anyone's death) you don't remember the pain or the violence of it...you remember the beauty of it**. The same is true with the passion narratives.

  - ◆ Mark was the first written down...and it is bloody... with vivid violent details.
  - ◆ Matthew gets more distant from the actual event, and so it gets more "theologized."
  - ◆ Luke's is even more distant and "theologized."
  - ◆ Then John, the last Gospel written, gets very distant from what actually physically happened to Jesus, and is the passion narrative theologized most of all.

THE PASSION NARRATIVE IN THE GOSPEL OF MATTHEW

At the death of Jesus, there is an apocalyptic event—with signs—illustrating God is breaking into history.

- Jesus is the fulfillment of Scripture...the Torah...the Pentateuch: Jesus is the new Moses.
- Ignatius uses Matthew because it was considered in his time to be "the Ecclesiastical Gospel."
- At the death of Jesus there is an earthquake...at the resurrection, there is an earthquake—again, an apocalyptic view of the world.
- Jesus is the new Moses: the true interpreter of the law, the ideal Jew, and the fulfillment of the law.
- Chapters 5 through 7 of Matthew express the teaching of the kingdom: Jesus came to establish His kingdom by His death.
- The trial of Jesus follows Mark's version.
- The crucifixion is portrayed as an apocalyptic event: the coming of God; a judgment of God; a visitation of God—powerful to the Jewish people...it is a theophany.
- There is a darkening; earthquakes; and the veil of the temple, a symbol of the covenant, is torn in two.
- Written in AD 85 and blaming the sacking of Jerusalem in AD 70 on the disbelief of the Jews for not accepting Jesus as Savior.
- The explanation of the guards at the tomb is to counter the story of the Jews.
- The entry into Jerusalem: I will destroy the temple, where the fig tree is a symbol of the people of Israel—bearing no fruit.
- Jesus's words from the cross are the same as in Mark.

THE PASSION NARRATIVE IN THE GOSPEL OF MARK

Mark's passion and resurrection narrative is the first written down—from Peter. It is the original "kerygma." The original Gospel is only Mark's few chapters of the passion and resurrection. All else in his Gospel is theologizing about the passion, death, and resurrection of Christ.

- The overriding theme of Mark is the aloneness and abandonment of Jesus—"My God, my God" (Ps 22). Read the whole Psalm 22, as it ends up positive and with hope.
- The messianic secret: a pagan centurion says, "Truly You are the Son of God"—a Gentile recognizes Jesus.
- A suffering Messiah…God triumphs by suffering.
- Mark was the first evangelist.
- Mark is a passion narrative with an introduction: sixteen chapters.
- Mark's whole Gospel is a cosmic battle between light and darkness.
- The messianic secret: only the demons and the centurion recognize Jesus.
- The secret of who Jesus is starts to come out:

  - As suffering.
  - Being alone.
  - Being abandoned.
  - See Isaiah 53.
  - See Psalm 22.
  - See Philippians 2.

- Chapters 12 through 16 are a rushing toward the passion.
- Mark's is a dark Gospel emphasizing the pain, suffering, desolation of Jesus.
- Jesus is continually unrecognized and misunderstood.

● The desolation of Jesus on the cross is centralized in Mark's passion narrative.

THE PASSION NARRATIVE IN THE GOSPEL OF LUKE

Luke emphasizes a forgiveness theme: the colloquy between the two thieves and Jesus.

● There is an inclusion of the marginalized throughout the whole Gospel.
● Luke has a more personal touch.

♦ Peter's healing of the soldier's ear at the arrest of Jesus.
♦ A movement from the Last Supper to the conversion of Peter.
♦ "I prayed for you, Peter, that you are not tempted."…
   As Philip is depicted in the *Last Supper* of Leonardo da Vinci.
♦ The good thief being acknowledged by Jesus.

● Luke–Acts is one-fourth of the New Testament, which gives us a picture of how Luke sees the importance of the death of Jesus, as foundational to Jesus's ministry.

♦ Part I: *infancy narrative*
♦ Part II: chapter 4, *Jordan experience* and *public life to the cross.* (Luke 9:51 says Jesus sets his face like flint toward Jerusalem.)
♦ Part III: Acts, *the period of the Holy Spirit in the Church*
♦ The passion: Luke dislikes violence—he leaves out the scourging—and in the agony, he glosses over the struggle and violence.
♦ There is no desolation.
♦ There is no apocalyptic sense.

- Luke is a passion of forgiveness:

  - "Father, forgive them for they know not what they do."
  - "Today you will be with Me in My kingdom" (good thief).

- The innocence of Jesus…before Herod…Jesus is a political football used for Pilate's and Herod's purposes.
- Jesus is treated as a nonperson with no rights at all, as many are treated in the world.
- The trust of Jesus in God's providence: "Into Your hands I commend my Spirit."
- Luke pays attention to the human qualities in Jesus's personal relationships.

THE PASSION NARRATIVE IN THE GOSPEL OF JOHN

The Gospel of John is the last Gospel written and, therefore, the most theologized about—and the most distant from the facts of the passion.

- The major theme of John is the GLORIFICATION…Jesus is glorified by His passion and by being crucified on the cross.
- Chapter 12, *the agony in the Garden*: wait and be empowered. Putting your entire being into God's hands gives you power—you are empowered.
- Jesus has command and control over all in John's passion narrative.
- In John, people choose an earthly king, Barabbas, over Jesus.
- In John's passion narrative, the Divinity is hidden, but Jesus is serene.
- For John, Jesus's "hour" is the crucifixion.

- The crucifixion is not shameful or horrible. It has a glory about it.
- The trial is like a Greek tragedy: a chorus, a crowd, long dialogues with Pilate; speaking from the cross, when in actuality someone dying on a cross could not speak.
- For John, the crucifixion has no abandonment, no horror. The only words are, "I thirst," and words to John and Mary and, at His death, "It is finished."
- Resurrection is not as important for John as his death: it is his "glorification."
- Also, "Woman, behold your Son," and to John, "Behold your Mother."
- Mary is in John, but not in the Synoptics.
- The Last Supper: John has five chapters for the Last Supper, chapters 13 through 17.
- For John, this is the BOOK OF GLORY.
- The HIDDEN MAJESTY OF GOD'S SELF-REVELATION IS IN JESUS.

PRE-NOTE: DIRECTION INVOLVEMENT DURING THE THIRD WEEK

- Third Week: see your people twice a day for support and encouragement. This is a time during the Spiritual Exercises where seeing retreatants twice a day is a possibility and needed perhaps.

  - Be open to it and suggest it, if necessary.
  - Example: a prisoner of war shares his war experiences with his wife. She is shaken. So Jesus shares His experience of his passion and death with us...what He went through for us. We are shaken. And our own life comes up as we look at Jesus.

- The LIFE OF CHRIST: A director takes on the brokenness, darkness, desolation, crucifixion, deprivation, disadvantages, flaws, and poverty of those we serve. This is an earmark of the ministry of Christ.

  ◆ So now the director experiences the loss, the suffering, and the humiliations of all the retreatants. There can therefore be in the director a certain heaviness, depression, an irritability, an impatience, an oversensitivity, an attitude. Take this in as a way to share the suffering of your retreatants.

  ◆ Actually, we don't have another model of ministry than Jesus: there is no other model of ministry than Jesus in the hymn of Philippians 2, taking on our darkness.

    His state was divine, yet He did not cling to His
       equality with
    God but emptied Himself to assume the condition of a
       slave,
    and became as men are, He was humbler yet, even to
    accepting death, death on a cross.
    But God raised Him high and gave Him the name
       which is
    above all other names so that all beings in the heavens,
       on the
    earth, and in the underworld, should bend the knee at
       the name
    of Jesus and that every tongue should acclaim Jesus
       Christ as
    Lord to the glory of God the Father. (Phil 2:6–11)

- You wonder if the pain, inability to pray, darkness, restlessness, distraction, and numbness you feel in and out of prayer now is "perhaps" Christ ministering and parceling out to you the pain of your retreatants. You may have to simply bring this in and suffer it.

- The director is going to have to "gut-up" here, to use street language.

HOW DO YOU GIVE THE THIRD WEEK OF THE SPIRITUAL EXERCISES?

Read aloud Annotation 15.

- Give an ASSORTMENT of all four passion narratives and let them pick which one with Christ.
- Give the major characteristics and themes of each of the four passion narratives, and let Christ call and move the retreatants to which to follow. Many retreatants don't know the differences of each passion narrative.
- Let Jesus take the lead and show the retreatant the pace of how many episodes there will be in the Third Week. So just be with Jesus. Go with Jesus where He goes. Jesus may not go through all the episodes. Jesus is the guide of this Third Week.
- Be careful that it is Christ who is leading the retreatants through the Third Week…not you, the director, but also not the retreatants themselves, as they may just be taking the most comfortable passion narrative or the most familiar one. Because "THE PROBLEM" could be—the one we want to avoid…that retreatants can be "self-protective" by choosing a comfortable passion narrative rather than letting Christ lead them.
- Go through the feelings of Jesus…guide and ask, "Can you get into the feelings of Jesus"?

  ◆ Stay with Jesus.

◆ Ask the retreatants, "Has someone you know died? What was that like for you? What was important in that experience for you?" Do that now in the Third Week.

◆ Call on your own experience and memories for some grieving event in your life.

◆ What was that like for you? Use what helps.

● Do the Third Week the way you did the Second Week. Use the same method…use the same fabric of procedure that worked for you during your Second Week.

● Bring back the Examination of Conscience. Ask what is the grace for you now in your Examination of Conscience?

● Give the *Anima Christi*.

● Give the Mount Tabor theophany: Luke 9:28–36.

● Do you have a favorite Gospel? Follow and stay with its passion narrative.

● Enter into a nonverbal gaze at Jesus on the cross.

● The Third Degree of Humility—turn it around…Christ wants to share our suffering…your suffering.

● How have you experienced the cross?

● Give the four *Servant Songs of Isaiah*: 42:1–9; 49:1–6; 50:4–9; 52:13—53:12.

● Give Romans 5:1–11. Christ died for us while we were still in sin.

● You cannot hold them back when they receive the grace.

● Parse out the retreatants' experiences to them. Feedback their experiences to them.

● Do the Stations of the Cross in the church or outside.

● The seven last words—first, read through the whole passion narrative that they choose.

● Paragraph 208: seven days in the third week.

● Paragraph 209: the Third Week may have more days in it…or fewer days.

- You do not have to have the retreatants do all the contemplations of the Third Week—they just have to get the grace of paragraph 193 and paragraph 203.
- Rules for scruples: paragraph 345

    ◆ These rules are very subtle.
    ◆ The over and over, back and forth kind of movement is a scruple and a temptation. Turmoil...compulsive thinking.
    ◆ Rule 6: This is a very contemporary and applicable rule:

        ▪ It is the biggest rule because of the issue of commitment: to marriage or to have children or to enter the priesthood or brotherhood, sisterhood or religious life.
        ▪ Because of contemporary psychology and counseling, we are aware of our imperfections and weaknesses— our pasts, and where this comes from in us. We are aware of our "impure motivation," "vainglory as the rule says"...or abandonment issues of fear that I'm not strong enough to make it.
        ▪ So, we need the rules for scruples more than ever.

- Interior Penance: paragraphs 82 and 89
- Sorrow for sins
- The third method of prayer: paragraph 238. What is it?

    ◆ What is the grace of the third method of Prayer?

        1) Simple prayer.
        2) A simple way.

    ◆ When do you use it?

        ▪ When someone is stuck.
        ▪ When the contemplations won't work.
        ▪ When their meditations won't work.
        ▪ When there is desolation or dryness, excessively.
        ▪ When retreatants are continually distracted.

▪ To focus thought when retreatants are wandering from one distracted thought to another.
▪ When retreatants are tired, resulting in an inability to focus on anything.
▪ When there is resistance and approach—avoidance about going into the passion: "It's like going into the subway…at the subway platform; I want to go—I don't want to go; I get on the subway, then I get off…next station—but it's all okay…the subway comes every ten minutes."

TO ONE WHO IS DIRECTING THE SPIRITUAL EXERCISES

What are you experiencing now within yourself?

- How does it make you feel?
- What is happening in your prayer now?
- How does it make you feel?
- How is your direction going?
- How does that make you feel?
- How are you giving the Third Week?
- How is Christ taking over the direction of the retreat in the Third Week? Also, the Act of the Presence of God and the Examination of Conscience?
- How are your retreatants making their way through the Third Week?
- How is your health?
- How is your prayer for your retreatants going?
- What is the gift of the Fourth Week of the Spiritual Exercises?
- What are the signs that a retreatant is asking for the Fourth Week of the Spiritual Exercises?
- How do you give the Fourth Week of the Spiritual Exercises?

FOURTH WEEK

Chapter 13

THE GRACE OF THE FOURTH WEEK OF THE SPIRITUAL EXERCISES

From the text of the Spiritual Exercises of St. Ignatius of Loyola:

218. FIRST CONTEMPLATION

The apparition of Christ our Lord to our Lady. # 299
   Prayer. The usual preparatory prayer.

219. FIRST PRELUDE. This is the history. Here it is how after Christ expired on the cross His body remained separated from the soul, but always united with the divinity. His soul, likewise, united with the divinity, descended into hell. There He sets free the souls of the just, then comes to the sepulcher, and rising, appears in body and soul to His Blessed Mother.

220. SECOND PRELUDE. This is a mental representation of the place. Here it will be to see the arrangement of the holy sepulcher and the place or house of our Lady. I will note its different parts, and also her room, her oratory, etc.

221. THIRD PRELUDE. This will be to ask for what I desire. Here it will be to ask for the grace to be glad and rejoice intensely because of the great joy and the glory of Christ our Lord.

222. THE FIRST, SECOND, AND THIRD POINTS. These will be the usual ones as presented in the contemplation on the Last Supper.

223. FOURTH POINT. This will be to consider the divinity, which seemed to hide itself during the passion, now appearing and manifesting itself so miraculously in the most holy Resurrection in its true and most sacred effects.

224. FIFTH POINT. Consider the office of consoler that Christ our Lord exercises, and compare it with the way in which friends are wont to console each other.

225. COLLOQUY. Close with a colloquy, or colloquies, as the circumstances suggest, and at the end say the *Our Father.*

NOTES

226. NOTE I. In the subsequent contemplations, all the mysteries from the Resurrection to the Ascension inclusive are to be gone through in the manner indicated below. As for the rest, throughout the whole Week of the Resurrection, let the same form be used and the same method observed as were followed during the entire Week devoted to the passion.

The first contemplation on the Resurrection, given above, will serve as a guide. The preludes will be the same, but adapted to the matter being considered. The five points will be the same. The Additional Directions will be as given below. In all the rest, for example, with regard to the repetitions, the Application of the Senses, the shortening or lengthening of the mysteries, etc., the Week devoted to the passion may serve as a model.

227. NOTE II. Ordinarily, it is more in keeping with this Week than with those that have passed to have four exercises a day instead of five.

In that case the first will be on rising in the morning, the second about the time of Mass, or before dinner, in place of the first repetition. The third, about the time of Vespers, will be in place of the second repetition. The fourth, before supper, will be the Application of the Senses to the matter of the three contemplations of the day.

In making the Application of the Senses, attention and more time is to be given to the more important parts and to points where the soul was more deeply moved and spiritual relish was greater.

228. NOTE III. Though in all the contemplations a definite number of points is given, say three, or five, etc., the one who is contemplating may make use of more or fewer as seems better for him. For this reason, it will be very useful before entering on the contemplation to foresee and determine a definite number of points that are to be used.

229. NOTE IV. In the Fourth Week a change is to be made in the second, sixth, seventh, and tenth Additional Directions.

The second will be, as soon as I awake, to place before my mind the contemplation I am to enter upon, and then to strive to feel joy and happiness at the great joy and happiness of Christ our Lord.

The sixth will be to call to mind and think on what causes pleasure, happiness, and spiritual joy, for instance, the glory of heaven.

The seventh will be, as far as there is reason to believe that it might help us to rejoice in our Creator and Redeemer, to make use of the light and the pleasures of the seasons, for example, in summer of the refreshing coolness, in the winter of the sun and fire.

The tenth will be, instead of penance, to attend to temperance and moderation in all, except on days of fast and abstinence ordained by the Church, which must always be observed if there is no legitimate excuse.

GOOD DIRECTION WITHIN THE CONTEXT OF THE SPIRITUAL EXERCISES OF ST. IGNATIUS: WHAT IS IT?

An example: The musician Father Don Osuna at the Oakland Cathedral in California says, "It is what we do not do that makes us successful." The musicians at the Oakland Cathedral all have master's degrees in music. At a moment's notice they could fill the whole cathedral with their music. But only occasionally did they do so. What they did was simply support the singing of the community.

From Ephesians 3:20: "Glory be to Him whose power, working in us, can do infinitely more than we can ask or imagine." This is what good direction is...plays for...wants.

STEP I

What is the grace of the Fourth Week of the Spiritual Exercises: Paragraph 221...the experience...the gift...the movement...the "work" of the Fourth Week of the Spiritual Exercises?

Read again paragraph 229. It amplifies 221.

THE MANY, VARIED ASPECTS OF THE GRACE OF THE FOURTH WEEK OF THE SPIRITUAL EXERCISES:

- The grace to be glad and rejoice internally because of the great joy and glory of Christ.
- A sense of empowerment over all evil with Christ my strength.
- A new way of presence.
- A point of integration...a release.
- A sense that Christ is with me no matter what.
- The true Christ is the victorious Christ.
- Concept of God changes from the Old Testament to the New Testament...Christ is Love and that is a different God than I have ever known before.
- The coming of the Kingdom...the Kingdom has come.
- The glory of the passion—a sense of meaning... *The Book of Glory*, as the Gospel of John would put it.
- The real Christ is the cosmic Christ...a world orientation.
- Depth—deep water runs deep. Not teenage joy but great joy: "Your sorrow will be turned into joy" (John 16:16–22).
- Sharing Jesus's perspective of joy...sharing that joy.
- Thank God, He is alive!
- Enjoying Jesus's friendship.
- The Joy of Christ is in that Jesus can do what He always wanted to do...spiritual indwelling—entering into the lives of people. As St. Ignatius says: "He consoles people in his resurrectional appearances...there is a recognition of who He is by those who see Him."
- As St. John Chrysostom says: "Those we love and lose are no longer where they were before. They are now wherever we are." This is spiritual indwelling—a new presence.
- As Jesus said at His Last Supper: "It is better for you that I go. You will grieve now but your sorrow will be turned into joy" (John 16:7).
- He means His new presence is better for us.

- Jesus now is present on every altar of his Eucharist as Priest and as Bread and Wine, His Body and Blood (see the book *The Eucharist of Jesus* by Robert Fabing)—a new presence.
- Jesus has come to his fullness of being…his full stature… who he really is. As when you see someone do what they've always wanted to do and can do—there is a glow about them.
- Look at the fifth point (paragraph 224): the grace of experiencing Christ as consoling…as consoler…to those to whom he appears.
- Hope in Christ.
- Christ is the New Moses…the new Exodus—he leads us out of the desert of death to new life.
- What you're looking for is resolution: Resolution is Resurrection.
- A deep peace under the retreatants' suffering…this peace is destroying a bad self-image.
- In probing into Jesus's joy, there is a sense that he can take you with Him.
- The retreatants are in joy because Christ is in joy.
- There is a new chance or a second chance sense…there is an opportunity…take advantage of it—enthusiasm. With Christ…a real resurrection.
- A sense of completeness.
- There is a new sense of healing.
- Whatever "the problem" was, it doesn't have you "by the neck" anymore—the problem is NOT "center stage" anymore…not self-absorbing…there is "freedom."
- I'm invited to walk through suffering and the death of Jesus into the consolation of life renewed and transformed, so that I stand with the Crucified and Risen Jesus as one who is consoled.
- Consolation is when we recognize the presence of God— Jesus's joy of a new life…his Resurrected Life.

- The Joy of Jesus in and from His resurrection: is like the joy of a father who buys and is taking home at Christmas or the birthday of his three-year-old son a tricycle to give to him...the father knows the joy that his son will have as his son sees the tricycle in front of the tree and then rides it. So the father has that joy himself in knowing how the child will react—this is the joy that Christ has at and in His resurrection as He knows the joy that that will bring us...as a father brings home a tricycle for His son, Christ has for us in anticipation—as He brings home the joy and freedom of his resurrection for us...it is His gift for us and to us. This is His joy in His resurrection that his gift for us in His resurrection...is that we have the freedom from all evil and from the fear of death forever, and that we will have the sure felt knowledge that we will live forever with Him—free from all evil and death...His JOY is that and His JOY will be ours.
- He hasn't done this just for Himself. He's done this for us.
- The depth of violence needs and requires a Tomb Day for us to absorb this gift.
- Honoring the depth of such a violent death and the emptiness of the loss is the occasion for a Tomb Day.
- There is such a thing as a "dispositional" resurrection that has to do with issues that Christ has brought up vis à vis today in the retreatants' life...so when they are resolved that IS a RESURRECTION...or an election or a reformation of life issue—and when the struggle is over, THAT IS THE RESURRECTION.
- In the Fourth Week grace, there is no "FOR ME" in Ignatius' words...as the grace to be prayed for in the first three weeks, so it is more joy with Christ that He has risen—all is on Him—however, Christ then reveals to the retreatants that He really has done this FOR THEM PERSONALLY.

- Jesus is not satisfied that all eyes are "on Him." Jesus is only satisfied when WE RISE WITH HIM. So, as we keep our eyes on Jesus in His resurrection, He raises us up...He gives us His resurrection—He resolves our dispositional issues here and NOW in the twenty-first century.
- The burden on me of saving myself is not on me alone anymore...Christ has lifted it by His resurrection.
- The grace of the Fourth Week only "begins" with eyes on Jesus—Jesus's Joy—because Jesus turns this focus onto us...the retreatants in the twenty-first century who have life issues now, and has the retreatants rise now in their lives: the resurrection is NOW.
- First Exercises: Jesus appears to His mother, Mary, first... Why? Because Mary is the First Disciple. Over Jesus's public life, Mary moved from being Jesus's mother to being Jesus's first disciple, the Mother of the Church NOW and forever—that is how it is that He appears to Mary first.
- Here in this particular movement of the Spiritual Exercises, the signs a person is asking the director for the Fourth Week are often THE VERY GRACE OF THE FOURTH WEEK ITSELF.

STEP II

The signs one is ready for the Fourth Week of the Spiritual Exercises:

A CONSTELLATION OF EXPERIENCES:

- One thinks of the glory of heaven.
- One is attracted to the glory of nature.
- One has thoughts of the victory of Christ.

    - Joy with Christ
    - A sense that they can go it alone now in the retreat

- There is a sense of meaning in the suffering of Christ.
- There is a sense of the hope and positivity of Christ in this.
- They see themselves or individuals in their lives as Christ on the cross…a sense of meaning—from the Application of the Senses.
- They look forward in their lives.
- The struggle with suffering and evil is over.
- The reformation of life or the election come back as good—the struggle with it is over…it comes back as a blessing.
- The ability arises to say the prayer of the Third Degree of Humility and mean it.
- There is nothing more—a sense of being satisfied.
- One has a sense that he or she can get something done in the world.
- Jesus wants to die because He wants to be with us in his resurrected presence.
- It is over…it is finished.
- When you can do what you could not have done before.
- I cannot sin enough to stop Christ's love for me.
- Body language: retreatants come bounding into the room.
- Director reads a sense of joy…one's own affect confirms retreatants' experience. The retreatants' joy is shared by the director. So, the director senses it in direction—before the retreatants do.
- You are free and you can now look ahead.
- "I have been to places that I have never been before…Jesus brought me there."
- "I was consoling Jesus and He started consoling me."
- "I brought up everything to God that I could think of (I don't want to end the retreat with unresolved issues, like old people in rest homes who are bitter and unresolved)… I'm at peace with everything."

- The passion is a private moment…an intimate gift given them by God.
- They change their attitude toward others in their lives—how wonderful they are—and their other problems no longer matter.
- There are thoughts of heaven and everlasting life.
- A spontaneous saying of the *Suscipe*: "Take, O Lord, my freedom…," which they could never say before and never wanted to say.
- Retreatants receive a simple gift of peace.
- They are embracing the suffering of Jesus.
- OH, HAPPY FAULT—*felix culpa*—my sin and the sin of all humanity comes back as not devastation but with joy… as a happy fault because of Christ's victory over sin and evil on the cross.
- One clearly sees that evil killed Jesus…powerfully… quickly…definitively.
- I have a new life…a whole new UNDERSTANDING… OUTLOOK on "myself…my problems…or issues."
- A release from the tension of the struggle with evil—with the Reformation of Life or whatever they have been dealing with in the retreat.
- When there is a dispositional resurrection, when the struggle—a NOW life issue for a particular retreatant is resolved—in peace…when a confirmation to a reformation of life issue or election has been confirmed, that is the resurrectional work of the Spiritual Exercises.

STEP III

How does St. Ignatius give the Fourth Week of the Spiritual Exercises? (Paragraphs 226 and 227)

- Ignatius offers them many and all of the resurrectional appearances of Jesus...and lets them pick their way through them, as they are led by their Creator and Lord: paragraphs 299–312.
- Focus on what Jesus's perspective is here.
- What is Jesus experiencing as He appears to those He Loves?
- Ignatius's first contemplation: Jesus's appearance to Mary—a wise choice. Who would you first appear to when you die? The one you love the most; for Jesus this is the First Apostle: Mary.
- Paragraph 224: Jesus, the Consoler...the Fifth Point.

STEP IV

How do you give the Fourth Week of the Spiritual Exercises? (We will not consider here the *Contemplatio Ad Amorem*.)

- Give it as simply as possible.
- Let them go through the resurrection accounts.
- Shifting into the experience and mind of Jesus...Jesus's perspective as He appears to the apostles.
- Have them get up early and see the sunrise.
- Give a tomb day: like a funeral, you remember the whole of the person's life: so in the tomb day, remember the whole retreat—the whole life, death, and resurrection of Christ.
- An unfinished grieving can come up here.
- With the new liturgical sense from the Second Vatican Council, people have a renewed experience of Holy Saturday as a real event, so plumb and use that.
- Explore a sense of what it would be like without Jesus...no Jesus.
- Linger as long as you need to with life memories of Christ's earthly life with you.

- Let the memories come up as they come up naturally…as a person is in a state of death shock—grieving.
- Do this tomb day with no specific formal prayer periods… just be with this all day.
- Just talk with Mary and Mary Magdalene and the apostles.
- What are Mary and Mary Magdalene going through?
- Prayer of reminiscence over the whole life of Jesus
- Always point out to the retreatants to ask and focus on what Jesus is experiencing: What is the perspective of Jesus as He appears to those He loves?
- Look at Raymond Brown's book *A Risen Christ in Eastertime: Essays on the Gospel Narratives of the Resurrection.*
- Paragraph 299: Appearance to Virgin Mary
- Jesus and Mary's intimate love
- This is not a privatized devotion.

What is Christ experiencing as he consoles each person in each of his resurrected appearances?

Chapter 14

THE CONTEMPLATION TO ATTAIN THE LOVE OF GOD

From the text of the Spiritual Exercises of St. Ignatius of Loyola:

230. CONTEMPLATION TO ATTAIN THE LOVE OF GOD

NOTE. Before presenting this Exercise, it will be good to call attention to two points:

1. The first is that love ought to manifest itself in deeds rather than in words.

231. 2. The second is that love consists in a mutual sharing of goods, for example, the lover gives and shares with the beloved what he possesses, or something of that which he has or is able to give; and vice versa, the beloved shares with the lover. Hence, if one has knowledge, he shares it with the one who does not possess it; and so also if one has honors, or riches. Thus, one always gives to the other.

PRAYER. The usual prayer.

232. First Prelude. This is the representation of the place, which here is to behold myself standing in the presence of God our Lord and of His angels and saints, who intercede for me.

233. Second Prelude. This is to ask for what I desire. Here it will be to ask for an intimate knowledge of the many blessings received, that filled with gratitude for all, I may in all things love and serve the Divine Majesty.

234. First Point. This is to recall to mind the blessings of creation and redemption, and the special favors I have received.

I will ponder with great affection how much God our Lord has done for me, and how much He has given me of what He possesses, and finally, how much, as far as He can, the same Lord desires to give Himself to me according to His divine decrees.

Then I will reflect upon myself, and consider, according to all reason and justice, what I ought to offer the Divine Majesty, that is, all I possess and myself with it. Thus, as one would do who is moved by great feeling, I will make this offering of myself:

TAKE, LORD, AND RECEIVE

Take, Lord, and receive all my liberty, my memory, my understanding, and my entire will, all that I have and possess. You have given all to me. To You, O Lord, I return it. All is Yours, do as You will. Give me only Your love and Your grace, this is enough for me.

235. Second Point. This is to reflect how God dwells in creatures: in the elements giving them existence, in the plants giving them life, in the animals conferring upon them sensation, in man bestowing understanding. So He dwells in me and gives me being, life, sensation, intelligence; and makes a temple of me, since I am created in the likeness and image of the Divine Majesty.

Then I will reflect upon myself again in the manner stated in the first point, or in some other way that may seem better.

The same should be observed with regard to each of the points given below.

236. THIRD POINT. This is to consider how God works and labors for me in all creatures upon the face of the earth, that is, He conducts Himself as one who labors. Thus, in the heavens, the elements, the plants, the fruits, the cattle, etc., He gives being, conserves them, confers life and sensation, etc.

Then I will reflect on myself.

237. FOURTH POINT. This is to consider all blessings and gifts as descending from above. Thus, my limited power comes from the supreme and infinite power above, and so, too, justice, goodness, mercy, etc., descend from above as the rays of light descend from the sun, and as the waters flow from their fountains, etc.

Then I will reflect on myself, as has been said. Conclude with a colloquy and the *Our Father*.

THE CONTEMPLATION TO ATTAIN THE LOVE OF GOD

What is the Grace of the Contemplation to Attain the Love of God?

- What are the signs a person is asking you to give them the Contemplation to Attain the Love of God?
- How do you give the Contemplation to Attain the Love of God?
- How did Ignatius give this?
- How do you give it?

STEP I

What is the Grace of the Contemplation to Attain the Love of God?

- In the Contemplation to Attain the Love of God, the grace is the same...similar—it is sensing Christ's giving me specific gifts—all from Christ—ponder how much He has given me of what He possesses: You have given ALL to me...so the focus is on Christ...what He is doing.
- Delight in surrender to Christ and coming back to myself as one who surrenders to the One who created me.
- A specificity in that I'm to serve God by receiving and using the gifts given to me...serve God in the gifts He has given to me personally—whatever gift your Creator has given you.
- Gifts given to the retreatant involve real suffering and labor...a bad self-image evanesces in this thanksgiving and in this self-abandoning into the gifts received from God.
- This is a relational grace—between God and the retreatants and all things—creating together.
- Seeing sin as a condition...not an identity...so God dwells in me: I am a temple of God.
- A mutuality in the Contemplation to Attain the Love of God between God and the retreatants.
- The Contemplation to Attain the Love of God is really Ignatian Contemplation as the Second, Third, and Fourth Week "eyes on Jesus" my life comes up...now MY LIFE IS SEEN AS GIFT—so I am given to myself by God as gift.
- This Contemplation is given to the retreatant to articulate what God is doing in the retreatant...what is going on and has been going on in the retreatant.
- This Contemplation clarifies the movement in the retreatant, like every spiritual exercise in the Spiritual

Exercises; they clarify the various movements in the retreatant—the movement of the Person who created the retreatant.

- We co-create the gifts given to us as well in that we use them well—we labor and suffer in them—we develop them...with God.
- God wants a relationship with the retreatant...an intimate relationship. God desires the retreatant.

    ◆ People don't feel desirable...people don't feel wanted... people have a bad self-image.
    ◆ God's desire for the retreatant relinquishes the hold on the retreatant of a bad self-image from within...from a deeper place within the retreatant.

GRACE: PARAGRAPH 233

Intimate knowledge of the blessings received, that filled with gratitude for all, the retreatants may in all things love and serve God.

The Contemplation to Attain the Love of God Sums Up the Entire Thirty-Day Retreat:	
First Point	First Week: Thanking God for creation
Second Point	Second Week: How God inserted God's life into creation
Third Point	Third Week: How God has labored and labors for the retreatant
Fourth Point	Fourth Week: How God gives all and has given all to the retreatant and how God has power over all

- Jesus did not raise Himself up from the dead but was raised up by God the Father to everlasting life.

- Jesus is given to Himself as raised up by His Father to ever-lasting life, just as in the Contemplation to Attain the Love of God, I am given to myself as gift by God.
- Christ was like us to the end: we do not raise ourselves from the dead, but we must be raised from the dead by Christ—so Christ experienced our lot by being raised from the dead by God the Father.
- This is now a shared experience between God and the retreatant…union with Christ laboring in the specific gifts that He has given me.
- This is the gift of "place me with Your Son," laboring in each specific gift that He has given the retreatant with Him laboring in each gift.
- Colossians 1: All of creation is one in re-creating reality—a new reality—bringing all back to God.
- God does this generosity…this generous giving…all of the time…all of my life…and has throughout all of human history.
- The *Suscipe*: Take, Lord, my freedom, take me and use me for ministry…a sharing in God's life.
- There is a sense realization that the retreatants' union with Christ laboring gives a sense of empowerment—gives the retreatants a grace of empowerment—a power…with Christ.
- There is a sense of participation with Christ in laboring in the gift to make it happen in the world…a very real participation in creativity with God…a sense of being a very real creator creating with the creativity of God. This brings to mind real JESUIT SPIRITUALITY here…Jesuit labor… Jesuit schools developing the gifts of our students… laboring—having our students practice, practice, practice: laboring.

  ◆ To receive God's love.
  ◆ To be aware of God's love.

- *Magis*: Do what you do with depth—a quality of my personal presence.
- God laboring…our work is God's work…in our laboring.
- We must be infected with loving as God loves us—we get our cue from how God loves us.
- The major insight is that most people have a "bad self-concept"…they have not been loved in their families and in their lives in a way that makes them feel like a "gift." Christ gives a person to themselves as "a gift" here. This destroys a bad self-concept…we are given in this grace to "imitate" the way Christ gives us everything freely—so this infects in us that same generosity—and in that allows us to say the *Suscipe* as the *Suscipe* is really the way that God gives everything to us:

> *Take, Lord, and receive all my liberty, my memory, my understanding, and my entire will, all that I have and possess. You have given all to me. To you, O Lord, I return it. All is yours, do as you will. Give me only your love and your grace, this is enough for me.*

STEP II

What are the signs one has finished the Fourth Week of the Spiritual Exercises?

What are the signs one is asking for and is ready for the Contemplation to Attain the Love of God?

- A retreatant realizes that this is the best day of the retreatant's life.
- Talking of how many good gifts the retreatant has received.
- A sense of the world.
- A sense of going out to the world.

- A sense of need to prepare to go out to world.
- If a retreatant feels they'd never want to leave the retreat.
- Fear of the future. Where is God?
- A sense of gratitude and integration.
- Joy with Christ joyful.
- Personalizing the resurrection: it is for me.
- I have risen in my life.
- A new life cycle…a new chance…coming up to live in the future.
- Their family members—loved ones keep coming up—the future…at home…or coworkers…or ministry…or ministry coworkers, or communities one lives and works with. This is not a distraction. It is a grace.
- "I love my work…ministry…I can't wait to get back to it in this new way."
- Thinking about all of the gifts they have received… throughout their whole life and/or throughout this retreat.
- Thinking about the Third Question of the Colloquy of the First Exercise of the First Week, "What can I do for Christ?" They are already here in the *Suscipe*. This comes back as gift.
- God is so good and so loving.
- The newness of beauty…I have looked at that tree or "whatever" all of the retreat and today I saw the beauty there.
- God was in my life all along, but I didn't see Him…didn't know that He was there.
- A sense that a tarnished relationship with Christ violates my relationship to Christ.
- A sense in the First Week that "I'm rotten and a sinner" to a sense that "I'm weak."
- What does one do with this joy?
- I want to give myself to God, and I'm excited to see what will happen.

The Contemplation to Attain the Love of God

Where is Jesus now…He went to "tell" His Mother that He is risen. It recapitulates the retreat.

Symphony Theme Again like Beethoven's 9th Symphony:	
First Principle and Foundation	POINT 1
The Kingdom Meditation	POINT 2
The Two Standards — the Three Degrees of Humility	POINT 3
Sentir: **The *Contemplatio ad Amorem***	POINT 4

STEP III

How did Ignatius give this Contemplation to Attain the Love of God?

- Ignatius gave the Contemplation to Attain the Love of God to people to pray on their way home from Paris to Rome when he gave them the Spiritual Exercises.
- Also, Ignatius gave the Third Method of Prayer for their journey home: paragraphs 238 and 258.

STEP IV

How do you give the Contemplation to Attain the Love of God? How do you give the Fourth week?

- Gerard Manley Hopkins's poem, "God's Grandeur"—to maintain the freshness of the Contemplation.
- 1 Corinthians 15—24, the resurrection theology
- Give one point of the Contemplation each day as a second prayer period after an appearance scene prayer period. This is because it is so overwhelming to take in one day. Also, if

you give it all at once a retreatant will not get to the Third or Fourth Points or give them enough time that they need.

- Give the Contemplation in one day: one point per prayer period over four formal prayer times in one day.
- Go through whole Contemplation with retreatants some days before the retreat ends and just ask them to take it as they feels moved to do so…letting Christ take the lead with them and moving them as Christ would wish.
- Give it with the "commissioning passages" in the Gospels—the sending out of the 72…the "go out to the whole world and baptize them in the name of the Father…" —laboring with Christ on mission…as in the kingdom (Luke 10:1–16).
- 2 Corinthians 5, "You are ambassadors of Christ."
- Acts 8:26–40, Christ sends apostles out: Philip to the Ethiopian (Acts 8:27)—now you are sent out to the world as an apostle.
- Psalm 138, A psalm of thanksgiving…when they have simple gratitude
- Psalm 116, "What shall I return to the Lord for all…I will give thanks."
- Psalm 8, God: the Creator of all

WHAT IS GOING ON IN YOU NOW AS A DIRECTOR?

- What are you experiencing now as you give the Fourth Week of the Spiritual Exercises?
- How is direction in the Fourth Week of the Spiritual Exercises different from direction in the First Week of the Spiritual Exercises?
- From your knowledge of the life of St. Ignatius, how do you experience the Spiritual Exercises as coming from him?

Chapter 15

ON CONCLUDING THE SPIRITUAL EXERCISES AND A RETREATANT'S ONGOING EXPERIENCE

CONCLUDING THE SPIRITUAL DIRECTION PROCESS

For the director:

- Let a retreatant feel that they are loved.
- Let a retreatant love you and let them thank you.
- Enjoy! This takes energy that we don't have: receiving, saying good-bye…receiving is God-like.
- Don't slough this off. This is important.
- Recognize grief…sorrow…depression at their leaving the retreat and a director leaving them and every one of us leaving the intense experience of the Spiritual Exercises.

The truth is the retreatant has done a lot for their director, and a director has done a lot for their retreatant.

Advice for the process of debriefing

In completing the full Spiritual Exercises of St. Ignatius in the direct thirty-day experience, to which this book has addressed itself, what would "debriefing" look like? Here are some possible suggestions, leaving room for your own imagination to supply more ideas.

This is number one—have them write down a self-statement: where are you today, thirty days later? Reflect on what they wrote down of where they were when they arrived: What I wrote down then: Where was I? Who was I? What has happened to me? What has God done? TRANSFORMATION IN THE RETREATANT—HOW DID THIS HAPPEN?

Go over the need for:

- The Act of the Presence of God.
- The Examination of Conscience.
- Daily prayer.
- Getting a spiritual director.
- Tell your spiritual director: "I need this or that." This is normal.
- Discuss spiritual reading: What is it? What is the place of the affections in spiritual reading?
- How do you share this transformative retreat experience with your spouse? With your community? With your own workplace?

  - Let them ask you how it was—THIS IS HOW YOU WILL BE HEARD THE BEST. It's like showing slides from your trip…it only goes so far before you lose people's interest.
  - LOOK FOR THE OPPORTUNITY of others asking you, "How was it?" Then tell them.

- Avoid romanticizing the retreat.
- Encourage your retreatants as the retreat ends.

- Focus on their return.
- Mission them out. Send them out. Bless them: "I know the plans I have for you, says the Lord, plans for good and not for disaster," Jeremiah 29:11–15; and Revelation 21.

To the director

What has been the grace for you in directing the Spiritual Exercises?

The gift of the experience of being used by God, and the feeling of not being needed: that is the experience of spiritual direction within the context of the Spiritual Exercises.

Do you experience the Spiritual Exercises as being a way to have great deeds born?

BIBLIOGRAPHY

ARTICLES

Althabegoity, Jean. "Confirmation: The Third and Fourth Weeks." *Centrum Ignatianum Spiritualitatis* 10, no. 3 (October 3, 1979): 87–95.

Aschenbrenner, George. "Becoming Whom We Contemplate." *The Way* 52 (1985): 30–42.

———. "Consciousness Examen." *Review for Religious* 31 (1972): 14–41.

Barry, William A. "The Experience of the First and Second Weeks of the Spiritual Exercises." *Review for Religious* 32 (January 1973): 102–9.

———. "The Spiritual Exercises and Social Action: The Role of the Director." In *Soundings*, 22–24. Washington, DC: Center of Concern, 1974.

Buckley, Michael J. "The Contemplation to Attain Love." *The Way*, Supplement 24 (1975): 92–114.

———. "Ecclesial Mysticism in the Spiritual Exercises of Ignatius." *Theological Studies* 56 (1995): 441–63.

———. "The Structure of the Rules for Discernment of Spirits." *The Way*, Supplement 20 (1976): 19–37.

Coreth, Emerich. "Contemplative in Action." *Theology Digest* 3 (Winter 1955): 37–45.

Cuenot, Claude. "Teilhard and the Spiritual Exercises of Saint Ignatius." *The Teilhard Review* 4 (1969/1970): 50–59.

Dhotel, Jean–Claude. "The Place of the Election." *Centrum Ignatianum Spiritualitatis* 10, no. 3 (October 3, 1979): 145–48.

English, John J. "Mysterious Joy of the Poor and the Complex Causes of Consolation." *Review of Ignatian Spirituality (CIS)* 85 (Rome, 1997): 74–75.

Kolvenbach, Peter–Hans. "The Spiritual Exercises and Preferential Love for the Poor." *Review for Religious* 43 (1984): 801–11.

Labarriere, Jean–Pierre. "The Christology That Is at Work in the Second Week." *Centrum Ignatianum Spiritualitatis* 10, no. 3 (October 3, 1979): 55–71.

Lewis, Daniel C. "The Exercise of the Kingdom in the Spiritual Exercises of St. Ignatius." *Review for Religious* 38 (1979): 566–70.

Lyonnet, Stanislas. "A Scriptural Presentation of the Principle and Foundation." *Ignis* 6 (1973): 24–32.

Malatesta, Edward J. "The Apostolate of the Spiritual Exercises." *The Way*, Supplement 24 (1975): 124–35.

Nigro, Armand. "God's Invitation." *Review for Religious* 65 (2006): 382–83.

O'Hanlon, Daniel J. "Zen and the Spiritual Exercises: A Dialogue between Faiths." *Theological Studies* 29, no. 4 (December 1978): 737–68.

O'Reilly, Terence. "Erasmus, Ignatius Loyola, and Orthodoxy." *Theological Studies* 30, no. 1 (April 1979): 115–27.

Padberg, John W. "Personal Experience and the Spiritual Exercises. The Example of Saint Ignatius." *Studies in the Spirituality of Jesuits* 10, no. 5 (November 1978): 245–333.

Peters, William. "St. Ignatius Loyola, Prophet." *Concilium* 4, no. 7 (1968): 15–23.

Veale, Joseph. "The First Week: Practical Questions." *The Way*, Supplement 48 (August 1983): 15–27.

———. "Ignatian Prayer or Jesuit Spirituality." *The Way*, Supplement 27 (Spring 1976): 5–7.

Yeomans, William. "The Two Standards." *The Way*, Supplement 1 (1965): 14–27.

BOOKS

Aschenbrenner, George. *Stretched for Greater Glory: What to Expect from the Spiritual Exercises*. Chicago: Loyola Press, 2004.

Balthasar, Hans Urs von. *Dare We Hope "That All Men Be Saved"? With a Short Discourse on Hell*. San Francisco: Ignatius Press, 2014.

Bangert, William V. *A Bibliographical Essay on the History of the Society of Jesus: Books in English*. St. Louis: Institute of Jesuit Sources, 1976.

Barry, William A., and William J. Connolly. *The Practice of Spiritual Direction*. New York: Seabury Press, 1982.

Brown, Raymond E. *The Death of The Messiah, From Gethsemane to The Grave: A Commentary on the Passion Narratives in the Four Gospels*. New Haven, CT: Yale University Press, 2014.

Byrne, Brendan. *Freedom in the Spirit: An Ignatian Retreat with Saint Paul*. Mahwah, NJ: Paulist Press, 2016.

Conwell, Joseph F. *Contemplation in Action: A Study in Ignatian Prayer*. Spokane: Gonzaga University Press, 1957.

Cusson, Gilles. *Biblical Theology and the Spiritual Exercises: A Method toward a Personal Experience of God as Accomplishing within us His Plan of Salvation*. St. Louis: Institute of Jesuit Sources, 1988.

de Caussade, Jean–Pierre. *Abandonment to Divine Providence*. New York: Doubleday, 2014.

Dister, John E., ed. *A New Introduction to the Spiritual Exercises of St. Ignatius*. Eugene, OR: Wipf and Stock Publishing, 2003.

Dyckman, Katherine Marie, and L. Patrick Carroll. *Inviting the Mystic, Supporting the Prophet: An Approach to Spiritual Direction*. Mahwah, NJ: Paulist Press, 1981.

Dyckman, Katherine Marie, Mary Garvin, and Elizabeth Liebert. *The Spiritual Exercises Reclaimed: Uncovering Liberating Possibilities for Women.* Mahwah, NJ: Paulist Press, 2001.

Egan, Harvey D. *Ignatius Loyola the Mystic.* Collegeville, MN: The Liturgical Press, 1991.

———. *The Spiritual Exercises and the Ignatian Mystical Horizon.* St. Louis: Institute of Jesuit Sources, 1976.

English, John J. *Spiritual Freedom: From an Experience of the Ignatian Exercises to the Art of Spiritual Guidance.* Chicago: Loyola University Press, 1995.

Fabing, Robert. *Deeper Than You Are.* St. Simons Island, GA: Kaufmann Publishing, 2015.

———. *The Eucharist of Jesus: A Spirituality for Eucharistic Celebration.* Portland: Oregon Catholic Press, 1986.

———. *Experiencing God in Daily Life: The Habit of Reflecting.* Portland: Oregon Catholic Press, 1992.

———. *Real Food: A Spirituality of the Eucharist.* Mahwah, NJ: Paulist Press, 1993.

———. *The Spiritual Life: Recognizing the Holy.* Mahwah, NJ: Paulist Press, 2004.

———. *With Roses for All.* St. Simons Island, GA: Kaufmann Publishing, 2012.

Fagan, Gerald M. *Putting On the Heart of Christ: How the Spiritual Exercises Invite Us to a Virtuous Life.* Chicago: Loyola Press, 2010.

Fleming, David L. *Draw Me into Your Friendship: A Literal Translation and a Contemporary Reading of the Spiritual Exercises.* St. Louis: Institute of Jesuit Sources, 1996.

———. *Like the Lightning: The Dynamics of the Ignatian Exercises.* St. Louis: Institute for Jesuit Resources, 2004.

Gallagher, Timothy M. *The Discernment of Spirits: An Ignatian Guide to Everyday Living.* New York: Crossroad, 2013.

———. *The Examen Prayer: Ignatian Wisdom for Our Lives Today.* New York: Crossroad, 2016.

———. *An Ignatian Introduction to Prayer: Scriptural Reflections according to the Spiritual Exercises*. New York: Crossroad, 2007.

———. *Meditation and Contemplation: An Ignatian Guide to Praying with Scripture*. New York: Crossroad, 2012.

Ganss, George E. *The Spiritual Exercises of Saint Ignatius: A Translation and Commentary*. St. Louis: Institute of Jesuit Sources, 1992.

———. *Total Development of the Jesuit Priest (Background Papers)*. Santa Clara, CA: University of Santa Clara Press, 1967.

Guibert, Joseph. *The Jesuits, Their Spiritual Doctrine and Practice: A Historical Study*. St. Louis: Institute of Jesuit Sources, 1994.

Hauser, Richard J. *Moving in the Spirit: Becoming a Contemplative in Action*. Mahwah, NJ: Paulist Press, 1986.

Ivens, Michael. *Understanding the Spiritual Exercises, Text and Commentary: A Handbook for Retreat Directors*. Leominster, Herefordshire, UK: Gracewing, 2016.

Manica, D. *Instruments in the Hand of God*. Rome: Gregorian University Press, 1963.

Martini, Carlo-Maria. *Letting God Free Us: Meditations on the Ignatian Spiritual Exercises*. Slough: St. Paul's Publications, 1993.

Munitiz, Joseph A., and Philip Endean, eds. *Saint Ignatius of Loyola: Personal Writings*. Penguin Classics. London: Penguin Books, 1997.

Olin, John C., and Joseph F. O'Callaghan, eds. *The Autobiography of St. Ignatius Loyola, with Related Documents*. New York: Fordham University Press, 1992.

O'Malley, John W. *The First Jesuits*. Cambridge, MA: Harvard University Press, 1993.

Osuna, Javier. *Friends in the Lord*. Translated by Nicholas King. London: The Way, 1974.

Palmer, Martin E. *On Giving the Spiritual Exercises. The Early Jesuit Manuscript Directories and the Official Directory of 1599*. St. Louis, MO: Institute of Jesuit Sources, 1996.

Puhl, Louis J. *The Spiritual Exercises of St. Ignatius.* Chicago: Loyola University Press, 1968.

Rahner, Hugo. *Ignatius, the Man and the Priest.* Rome: Centrum Ignatianum Spiritualitatis, 1982.

———. *Ignatius the Theologian.* Translated by Michael Barry. London: Geoffrey Chapman, 1968.

———. *The Spirituality of St. Ignatius Loyola: An Account of Its Historical Development.* Translated by Francis J. Smith. Chicago: Loyola University Press, 1980.

Rahner, Karl. *Saint Ignatius of Loyola.* New York: Collins Publishing, 1979.

———. *Spiritual Exercises.* London: Sheed and Ward, 1980.

Stanley, David M. *I Encountered God.* Edited by George E. Ganss. St. Louis, MO: Institute of Jesuit Sources, 1985.

———. *A Modern Scriptural Approach to the Spiritual Exercises.* St. Louis, MO: Institute of Jesuit Sources, 1994.

Toner, Jules J. *A Commentary on Saint Ignatius' Rule for the Discernment of Spirits.* St. Louis: Institute of Jesuit Sources, 2002.

———. *Discerning God's Will: Ignatius of Loyola's Teaching on Christian Decision Making.* St. Louis: Institute of Jesuit Sources, 1991.

Veltri, John. *Orientations. Vol. 2, For Those Who Accompany Others on Their Inward Journey.* Guelph, Ontario: Loyola, 1998.

Wall, Joseph B. *The Providence of God in the Letters of St. Ignatius.* San Jose, CA: Smith–McKay, 1958.

APPENDIX

Suggested Scripture Texts for Use in Directing the Spiritual Exercises of St. Ignatius of Loyola

Please Note: topics for each week are in the order of how the Exercises progress.

FIRST WEEK

First Principle and Foundation: Gen 1:26–31; 22:1–18; Deut 7; Wis 9:1–18; Matt 13:44–46; Luke 9; John 12:25; Col 1:15–20

God's Invitation: Ps 65:1–11; Isa 55:1–13; Jer 1:4–10; Matt 11:28–30; Mark 6:30–44; John 14:1–15; Rev 3:14–22

Give Thanks to the Lord: Pss 100:1–14; 147:1–20; Matt 15:32–38; Luke 17:11–19; Eph 1:3–10; 2 Thess 5:16–18; 1 Tim 2:1–4

Presence of God: 2 Macc 7:5–6; Pss 116; 139; 1 Cor 13:12; 2 Cor 2:17; 3:16–18

Sin in the World: Gen 3:1–13; 42—43; Ezek 28; John 8:44;
  1 John 3:8; Rom 1:18–32; 5:6–21

Sinfulness of Humanity: Gen 3:1–24; Pss 50:1–23; 82:1–8;
  Ezek 16; Hos 2:4–25; 11:1–11; Rom 1:18–32

Personal Involvement in Sin: Ezek 37; Matt 18:1–35;
  Rom 7:14–25; 8:19–23; 1 John 1:5—2:2

My Own Personal Sinfulness: Pss 38:1–23; 51:1–21;
  Matt 22:1–14; Luke 14:16–24; Rom 7:13–25;
  Gal 5:13–22; 1 John 2:1–11

God Is Speaking to Me: Matt 13:1–23; John 1:1–14;
  Rom 10:8–17; 2 Thess 2:13–17; 2 Tim 3:14–17;
  1 John 1:1–16

God's Love; How God Loves People: Isa 5:1–7; Jer 31:3; Hos
  11:1–6; Rom 11:28–29; Heb 1:1–4

God—Consistent and Constant throughout History:
  Isa 52:13; Jer 51:3; John 3:14; 8:28; 12:32

For Confession: Pss 32 (penance); 63; 85 (forgiveness);
  Sir 5:4–10

Conversion: Isa 30:15; Jer 25:5–7; Ezek 33:10–20;
  1 Thess 1:45

The Spirit in the Old Testament: Sir 44:1–15;
  Ezek 36:25–29; 37:1–14; 1 Thess 1:5

Secret Unveiling: Isa 48:6–7

God's Otherness…Uncontrolled…Free: 1 Thess 2:13–14

On Judging Others: 1 Cor 4:5

Troubles; Being Unsettled: Prov 9:7–11; 10:12; 11:1–6; 12;
  13:1; Rom 16:17–20; 1 Cor 1:10ff.; 3:1—4; 5:9–13;
  Gal 1:1–10; 5:13–26; Eph 4:14–16; 5:1–14;
  Phil 3:17—4:1; Col 3:5–11; 1 Thess 3:1–5; Jas 5:13–18

Hell: Matt 1:28; 5:22; 13:24–30, 36–43; 23:23; 25:41–46;
  Luke 16:19–30; John 3:16–21; Rev 20:11–15

Listening: A Way to God: Jer 13:1–11

Wonder and Reverence: Pss 84; 91; 145; 147; 149;
  Sir 16:17–22, 27; Eph 1:1–14

Appendix

Heart: Ps 63; Isa 29:13–14; Jer 20:74; 29:11–14;
  Ezek 11:18–19; 36:25–29; Rom 2:12–24; 10:8–13;
  John 17:15–19; Heb 9:9–10
Fasting—Good Works: Isa 58:1–12
Anger against God: Jer 15:10, 18; 20:17
Liturgical Prayer: 1 Tim 2:1–8
Sacred and Secular: Acts 10:9–16
God Searches for You: Jer 23:23–24; Amos 9:1–4;
  1 Thess 5:1–3; Heb 4:12–13; 9:9–10
Holiness: 2 Cor 1:12–22; 1 Thess 4:1–12
All Is Vanity but God: Lev 26:27–40; Eccl 2; Rev 18:11–24
Prayer: Ps 63; Prov 10:14; Luke 11:1–13; Rom 8:26–28;
  Eph 3:14–21; Phil 1:3–11
God's Message versus Human Thinking: Rom 1:18–25;
  11:33–36; 1 Cor 1:26–31; 2:1ff.; Gal 1:1–2, 11–12;
  2:6–8, 20–23; 1 Thess 2:13–16; 1 Tim 1:3–7; 6:3–5,
  20–21; 2 Tim 2:14–18
Weakness: Rom 8:26; 1 Tim 1:12–17
God Is Life: Isa 25:1–5; Mic 5:4a; Zech 2:1–5
Death: 1 Cor 15:12–19, 28, 48–49; Phil 1:20–26;
  1 Thess 4:12–18; Heb 2:14–18; 6:1–2
Purity of Intention: Ps 63; 2 Cor 2:17; Jas 3:13–18
Wisdom of God: Ps 33:10; Wis 7:7–14; Isa 29:14; 53:18;
  Jer 9:22–23; Bar 3; 1 Cor 1:19; 3:19–23; Jas 3:13–18
Evil People Prosper: Job 21:1–34; Ps 73; Prov 29:7
Hope: Pss 33:18–19; 34:17–20; 35; 57; 62; Sir 11:12–30;
  Isa 40:27–31; 46:12–13; Rom 4:18–25; 8:18–25;
  1 Tim 4:7–11; Heb 11
Salvation History: Neh 9; Pss 68; 78; 105; Jdt 5:5–24;
  Wis 10:1–19, 22; Sir 44:1—50:31; Bar 1:16—3;
  Ezek 16; 17; Acts 7; Eph 1:3–14; Heb 11
Nothingness of Idolatry: Lev 26:27–40; Job 8:8–22;
  Wis 13:10–19; Isa 2:6ff., 9–18; 3:1–15; 31:1–3; 44:9–20;
  45:20–22; Jer 14:10; 18:13–17; Ezek 13:1–16; 14:1–11;

Hos 8:8–13; 9:10; 12:1–3; 13:1–4; Amos 6:1–7;
Rev 19:5–10

Discerning the Spirit: Job 33:1–30; Pss 77; 88; 94:12–13;
Prov 2:1–9; 10:28; 11:3; 29:27; 1 Cor 14:32–33, 26–33;
2 Cor 3:16–18; Eph 4:17–24; Heb 6:1–2; Jas 3:13–18;
1 Pet 4:1–2

SECOND WEEK

Satan: 1 Cor 5:4; 2 Cor 11:7–15; Eph 6:10–20;
1 Thess 2:17–20; 2 Thess 2:33—3:12; Jas 3:13–18

Poverty...and Generosity: Ps 52; 2 Cor 8:6–15; 9:6–15;
Rev 18:11–24

Forgiveness: Ps 85; Prov 10:12; Sir 11:12–30; Rom 11:11–15,
29; 2 Cor 2:5–11; 5:16–21

Prayer Group on Forgiveness: Service with Christ in Love:
Pss 85:1–3, 8; 89:1–2, 17–21, 34–35; John 13:2, 4–5,
12–15; Rom 8:9–11; 11:29; 2 Cor 5:16–21

God Saying "I Love You": Pss 139; 145:1–21; Isa 43:1–5;
49:1–6; 62; Jer 31:31–34; Ezek 34:11–16; John 3:16–18

Call of Yahweh: Isa 6; 8:11; Jer 1:1–19; 15:15–21; 20:7–18;
23:35; Ezek 16:3–16; Jonah 1; Heb 11

Trust in Providence: Luke 12:22–32

Discerning the Spirit: Job 33:1–30; Pss 77; 88; 94:12–13;
Prov 2:1–9; 10:28; 11:3; 29:27; 1 Cor 14:26–33;
2 Cor 3:16–18; Eph 4:17–24; Heb 6:1–2; Jas 3:13–18;
1 Pet 4:1–2

Prayer Group: Personal Love of God for Us: Isa 40:27–31;
55:1–4; Ezek 11:18–19; Hos 11:3–4; Rom 8:31–39;
1 John 4:4

Listen to Jesus Say "I Love You": Matt 6:25–34;
John 15:1–13; 17:20–26; Rom 8:28–39; Eph 2:1–10;
1 John 3:1–2; 4:7–19

Call of the Kingdom: Matt 9:35—10:42; John 1:14–51;
   Rev 21—22

Kingdom of God Is Power; A State of Being: Lev 26:27–40;
   1 Cor 4:19–20

Person of God over All Else: Ps 63; John 5—12;
   Rom 8:31–39; 1 Cor 2:15–17; 3:22; 4:1–11; 5:1–6;
   7:32–35; 15:20–28; Phil 3:6–16; 4:10–12; Col 5:1–6;
   Rev 19:5–10

Incarnation Meditation: Ps 14

Servant: 1 Cor 3:1–11; 4:1–13; 2 Cor 3:1–11; 6:3–10;
   Gal 5:13; 6:1–5; Eph 3:1–13; Phil 2:3–11; 1 Tim 1:12–17

Covenant: 1 Chr 17:16–27; Isa 55:3–5; Jer 24:1–11; 31:3,
   31–34; Bar 3:7–8; Ezek 16:39–63

Israelite Pride and Questioning of Yahweh: Num 14:11–19;
   Deut 1:24; Ps 77; Jer 18:13–17; Bar 1:16—3; Ezek 28

Friendship: Sir 6:14–17

Bringing up Children: Sir 30:1–13

Sex and Marriage: 1 Cor 7:1ff.

Deserting God Yields "Smoke" and Confusion:
   Lev 26:27–40; Job 8:8–22; Bar 1:16—3

Teaching Jesus…God: Rom 1:3–7; 9:6–13; 1 Cor 2:13ff.;
   3:5–9

The Body of Christ: Rom 12:8–13; 1 Cor 12:12–30;
   Eph 2:19–22; 4:1–6; 5:29–33

Life…God…Choose Life: Deut 30:15–20

Lord as Comforter and Strengthener: Pss 34:17–20;
   53:18–19; 63; Sir 11:12–30; Rom 3:1–6; 2 Cor 1:3–8;
   2 Thess 2:13–17

The Father Knows Me and Loves Me: Ps 139; 1 Cor 13:12;
   2 Cor 1:3–4; 13:3–4

Prayer Group: The Joy of Trusting Yahweh: Ps 63;
   Isa 46:8–13; Phil 1:3–11; 2 Tim 1:6–9

Two Standards Exercise: Matt 14:1–21; Mark 6:17–29;
 Luke 6:20–49; Gal 5:16–26; Eph 6:10–20; 2 Thess 2:4–12;
 Rev 12:18—22:5

The Spirit in the New Testament: Sir 44:1–15; Rom 1:26–52;
 8; 1 Cor 2:10–16; 12:1–11; 13; 14:20–25; Gal 3:3–9, 21;
 5:16–26; Eph 4:9–13; Heb 9:9–10; Jas 3:13–18

Love: Rom 9:22–24; 12:14–21; 13:8–10; 14; 15:1–13;
 1 Cor 8:1–3; 13; 14:1; 16:13–14; 2 Cor 2:4; 7:2–4;
 12:11–15; Eph 4:1–6; Phil 1:3–11; Col 2:1–2; 3:12–15;
 1 Thess 5:12–18

Generosity of God: Sir 29:8–17; Heb 1:1–4

Joy—Praise—Exult: 1 Chr 16:8–36; 1 Thess 3:11–13;
 Rom 16:25–27

Blood Sacrifice—Blood of the Covenant: Exod 24:8

Speak Out—Courage—For What Is Ours—Truth:
 Rom 1:16; 8:31–39; 2 Cor 4:1–6; 10:8

Freedom: 2 Pet 2:19–21

Rich or Poor: Sir 13:21–52

Justice: Ps 82; Jer 12; 22:13–17

Faith in Jesus Christ—the Source: Pss 42; 43; 59:10,
 16–17; 62; 63; 71; Sir 11:12–30; Rom 4; 1 Cor 3:10–15;
 7:29–31; 2 Cor 10; 11:1–3; 13:5; Gal 3:23–29;
 Eph 1:15–25; Phil 3:6–16; Col 1:15–20

Despair: Pss 35; 38; 55; 88; 142; 143; Jer 45:3; 50:7;
 Bar 1:16—3; 2 Cor 6:3–10; 7:8–12; Col 1:24–29

How to Shepherd: Jer 23:1–8; Ezek 34

Work of the Father: Rom 5:7; 8:28, 30; 2 Cor 5:11–21

Yahweh's Promise to David and to Solomon: 1 Sam 7:10–16;
 2 Sam 7; 1 Kgs 9:1–10; 1 Chr 17:16–27; Mal 3:1–5

God's All-Embracing Totality in Grace: 1 Cor 15:6–8;
 2 Cor 5:14; Eph 2:7–10; 1 Thess 1:45

God Wants You, Not Sacrifice: Isa 1:11; Hos 6:4–6

Light: Isa 60:19–20; Mic 3:5–8; Rom 13:11–14;
 Col 1:12–14

Listen to God Speaking through the Word: Isa 55:1–13; 95:1–11; Jer 1:4–10; Matt 11:28–30; Mark 6:30–44; John 14:1–15; Rev 3:14–22

God's Mercy: Ps 51:1–21; Sir 18:1–13; Isa 1:15–18; Jer 32:36–41; Ezek 36:25–27; Joel 2:12–17; Mark 2:1–12; Luke 7:36–50; 15:1–7, 11–32; John 8:3–11; 10:1–19; 21:15–17; Heb 10:1–18

The Desert: Bar 1:16—3

Suffering: Job 3:24–26; 10:1–10; Pss 38; 55; 69; 103; 140—41; Rom 8:17–27; 2 Cor 7:8–12; Col 1:24–29; 1 Tim 1:12–17; Heb 2:8–12; 12:5–13; 1 Pet 4:12–18

Vatican II Documents: (2) Religious Freedom; (4) Ecumenism; (37) In the Church; (59) Church Today; (80) Church Today; (93) Church Today Building the Earth

THIRD WEEK

Jesus Weeps: Matt 24:37–39; Luke 7:11–17; 19:41–44; John 11

The Cross: Deut 21:22–23; Isa 10:22; 1 Cor 1:17ff.; Gal 2:18–21; 3:13–14; Col 2:14–15

God Is Speaking to Me: Matt 13:1–23; John 1:1–14; Rom 10:8–17; 2 Thess 2:13–17; 2 Tim 3:14–17; 1 John 1:1–16

He Who Spreads Grief and Sorrow: Job 5:6–7

Suffering: Job 3:24–26; 10:1–10; Pss 38; 55; 69; 103; 140—41; Rom 8:17–27; 2 Cor 7:8–12; Col 1:24–29; 1 Tim 1:12–17; Heb 2:8–12; 12:5–13; 1 Pet 4:12–18

God's Power—Our Weakness—Trust: Exod 4:10–17; Lev 26:27–40; Eph 2:7–10; 3:14–21; Phil 4:10–12; 1 Thess 1:4–5; 2 Tim 1:6–9; 4:16–18; *See* Jerusalem Bible at Rom 3:24 for footnote I on "grace"

Scandalizing: Sir 28:13–30; 1 Cor 8:7–13

Eucharist: 1 Cor 10:14–22; 11:17–34

FOURTH WEEK

The Risen Lord: Isa 54:4–10; Matt 28:1–10; Acts 2:29–36;
Rom 6:3–11; 1 Cor 15:20–28, 35–58; Col 3:1–11;
resurrection accounts

Contemplation: Job 9:3–9; 38; 39:5–12, 18–30; Pss 65:6–7;
74:7, 15; 104; Sir 42:15–43; 43:8–9, 27; 44:1–15;
Heb 3:1–5

Wonder and Reverence: Pss 84; 91; 145; 147; 149;
Sir 16:17–22, 27; Eph 1:1–14

Petrine Authority: Isa 22:22

Community Life: Rom 12:8–13; 1 Cor 14:1–12;
2 Cor 2:14; Eph 4:1–6; 1 Thess 5:12–15

The Church—a Sacrament to All People: 2 Chr 6:32–34;
Jer 1; Zech 8:20–23; Acts 10:44–48; 11:17; 15:7–12;
Rom 2:12–16; 3:21–26; 9:1–29; 11:11–24; 1 Cor 3:4–6;
14:36–37; Eph 3:1–13

WORKS BY THE AUTHOR

Father Fabing's work has been translated into Spanish, Italian, Polish, Japanese, Korean, and Chinese.

BOOKS

Deeper Than You Are
Discipleship in Christ: Growing in Daily Spirituality
The Eucharist of Jesus: A Spirituality for Eucharistic Celebration
Experiencing God in Daily Life: The Habit of Reflecting on Love,
    Joy, Need, Fear, Sorrow, and Anger
Real Food: A Spirituality of the Eucharist
The Spiritual Life: Recognizing the Holy
With Roses for All

In addition, Father Fabing is the senior architect for *The New Catechism: Finding God, Grades 1–8*.

LITURGICAL MUSIC COLLECTIONS

Adoramus
Be Like the Sun
Come All People
Everlasting Covenant

WORKS BY THE AUTHOR

Indwelling
Let Me Follow
Mass for Teresa of Calcutta
Only Your Love
Seeking You
Shadow of My Wings
Song of The Lamb
Windowpane
Winter Risen
Your Love Is More Than Life Itself
Your Song of Love

ABOUT THE AUTHOR

Father Robert Fabing, SJ, founded the 36-Day Program in the Spiritual Exercises of Saint Ignatius Loyola at the Jesuit Retreat Center in Los Altos, California, where he lives. He ran the program for nearly forty years, during which time there were usually sixty-one retreatants and seventeen directors. He also founded the Jesuit Institute for Family Life, which grew in the ensuing years as he founded eighty-seven marriage counseling and family therapy centers worldwide, named the Jesuit Institute for Family Life International Network. Father Fabing writes liturgical music and has recorded twenty-eight albums of his original liturgical music.